The Sewing Connection
Series 14

D1385020

• 922 Cheltenham Way • Plainfield, IN 46168 •
1-800-237-4475

Printed by Paramount Printers Ltd.
Lethbridge, Alberta, Canada

Many, many thanks to:

David Larson Productions
5910 North Lilly Road
Menomonee Falls, Wisconsin 53051

Producers:	Dave and Kate Larson
Director:	Ivy Lynn Chapman
Editor:	Pete Pfankuch
Engineer:	Ken Esmeier
Production:	Mike Geraci, David C. Larson, Dan Quinn, Tom Reardon, Mark Schwerin, Andy Steiber
Stylist:	Luella Doss
Models:	Luella Doss, Kathy Fuerstenau, Jennifer Crinello, Pat Fischer, Evelyn Klug, Elizabeth Shew, Maribel Steiber

My production assistants in Lethbridge:

Patricia Bunn
Bob Gregson and the fine staff at
    Paramount Printers Ltd.
Lynn Gregson, artist, Celebration Cards Ltd.
Sheila Matson
Cablenet 12

**A grateful acknowledgement to these quality companies for partial
underwriting of the television series:**

Bonfit America
5811 Uplanderway
Culver City, CA 90230
1-800-5-BONFIT

*The professional adjustable pattern
for all sizes, all styles.*

Coats and Clark
30 Patewood Drive, Suite 351
Greenville, SC 29612
(803) 234-0331

*America's number one name in
sewing and needlecraft*

New Home/Janome
Sewing Machine Company
10 Industrial Avenue
Mahwah, NJ 07430
(201) 825-3200

*Delightful machines with which you can
"make it special".*

FISKARS®

Fiskars Inc.
7811 West Stewart Avenue
Wausaw, WI 54401
(715) 842-2091

*Innovative makers of scissors,
rotary cutters, blades, cutting mats -
tools for every conceivable cutting project.*

Sewing Connection – Series 14

Think 3-D - Quilted clothing and accents featured in this section. Many tips and techniques are discussed.

Make gorgeous accessories or entire garments with fantasy fun fur from Donna Salyers. Give an existing coat new life.

Treat the special loom woven fabrics to create outstanding garments. Start to finish methods are discussed in this section.

Here is your chance to explore your artistic sewing skills. The New Home Memory Craft 9000, your favorite Coats and Clark threads and special embellishments, teamed with the clutch pattern, give outstanding results.

Crazy quilt techniques that can be used in garments. Use silks and other beautiful fabrics combined for a one of a kind look. Bring many pieces in your wardrobe together.

Celebration in Pink   # Chapter 1

Welcome back to series 14 of The Sewing Connection. I'm Shirley Adams and I'm just delighted to be here with you again. I've been all over the continent, exposed to all manner of wonderful inspiration, and am here to bring some of this back to you.

Wherever I travel people are so nice. Sewers are terrific humans as I have always known, but now we have scientific proof to back this fact. An intensive study proves that sewing is a hobby with one of the biggest stress relieving bonuses. Blood pressure actually decreases appreciably as you sit and sew; your troubles melt away. I love my sewing machine.

This is Celebration in Pink as you see in the suit I am wearing on the cover. What are we celebrating? Weddings? Happily ever after is what I wish for everyone so inclined. What is on this suit has been lifted from Japanese kimono. These were rentals I am told by the woman from whom I purchased the panels. They were parts of beautiful silk kimono that had been used and cleaned repeatedly until they were no longer wearable. At that point they were cut apart and the embroidered parts saved for further use. These panels could be lovely framed and displayed on a wall. I chose to cut out the embroidery and appliqué it to the jacket, as its original background fabric looked dreadful. However, the metallic embroidery is still lovely.

When cutting out something like this, be careful about those edges. I wanted to cut as closely as possibly so none of the old fabric remained, but great care must be taken to avoid cutting any of the embroidery thread. A seam sealant around the edge can be a good idea. Again, proceed with caution to avoid discoloration and stiffening. Try first in a small area to see what will happen.

I found definite discoloration on the fabric, but not on the embroidery thread. Since that would not matter with its being cut away, I tried other brands to see which might work best.

The greater problem here was the stiffness that the sealant produced. For this reason also, I suggest you use as little sealant as possible. When it is completely dry, before cutting out, rub these edges against each other slightly to see if you can soften it. If the stiffness will be objectionable on the garment to which it will be applied, avoid the sealant and just cut with the utmost care.

Since it was a large panel, the next decision you must make is to either use it in its entirety or cut sections apart. As a whole it would extend over the shoulder and partially down the back of the jacket. However, this would use up the whole piece in a concentrated area, and leave nothing for the left side. The other option is to cut parts off and cross over to the left front (entirely possible since there is a little daylight between some of flowers). Cut nothing until you are absolutely sure as you want no later regrets. For this decision-making procedure, cover the panel with a sheet of wax paper and trace all the flowers. Cut this apart, and position on your garment for best placement.

Appliquéing the embroidered flowers

It is crucial that you not blunder on something valuable. Practice first on flowered fabric by pressing a fusible sheet on the backside of a print fabric. Carefully cut out the flow. Peel off the backing paper. Fuse this to a firm fabric in a solid color. The stitching technique is what you will practice until you can do this well.

In trying to achieve a natural look when appliquéing objects from nature such as flowers and leaves, blending is very important. A stiff satin stitch around the edge doesn't work well at all. Instead, it should softly feather the edges so that the thread seems to be part of the embellishment.

Sherree Dawn Roberts is an international specialist in her teaching of decorative thread usage. Her Web of Thread shop in Kentucky boasts about every thread available. Sherree offers this tip:

"Rather than satin stitching perpendicular to the

leaf edge, stitch in the direction of the leaf point or tip. Set your machine on a fairly wide zigzag and drop the feed dog. Change to an embroidery foot for greater mobility in free motion stitching. Clamp your flower-fused fabric in a hoop or place some stabilizer under it so that the thread won't draw up in the project, but stay flat. You may or may not have to loosen the upper thread tension slightly but you'll find that out as you practice on this scrap."

Another determinant is the thread. Matching thread or microfilament nylon will be the least noticeable. Try a little of each and compare to judge which is better. Start stitching at the leaf base and progress toward the tip, then back on the other leaf edge to the base again. The new Coats and Clark twist embroidery thread, in a blend of 2 colors, is available to try.

For pivoting so frequently a knee lift on my Memorycraft 9000 is wonderful and really simplifies the job. If you're in the market for a machine, look for this feature.

As you practice you may find this works very well with a standard zigzag. Another possibility would be a shading stitch. This is one that is straight on one side but varies for better blending on the other side. If you have this capability on your machine, try it also 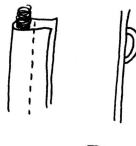 to find the best alternative. A little practice will find you doing a professional job appliquéing the edges with a natural look. Then you'll be ready to work on the actual project

This was the general procedure I used with my pink jacket, on which the silver embroidery is appliquéd. I cut out the jacket pattern pieces in a wool crepe and fused interfacing to the backside. The appliqué was done before constructing the suit, while the pattern pieces were still flat.

Cutting pieces of the traced design out from waxed paper, and arranging them in various ways on the fronts took the fear or apprehension out of doing this. Looking at the complete panel was scary, because of the thought of making a mess and ruining it all. Breaking the process down into components and practicing on scraps gives you the answers to all your questions. You can then proceed confidently.

I do things like this with every project. No one knows the answer to every question. You discover procedures heretofore unknown, and become more accomplished as you practice.

I saved some appliqué until later. Because a section was going over my left shoulder, I left the top flower loose until after the shoulder seam was stitched and pressed. On the right hip band some needed to wrap around into the back. This I also folded back out of the way until the seam was completed, then I appliquéd. Ensure that everything fits perfectly before appliquéing because once a seam is covered over with the embellishment it cannot be altered.

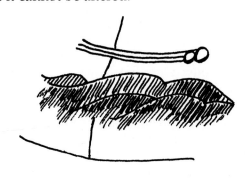

Pretty little finishing touches also make a project more special, more valuable. A satin piping filled with yarn is stitched on the jacket edge before the facing is applied. Bias tubes for buttonloops are created at the same time since they would look better than buttonholes. The little buttons used were chosen because they looked exactly like the silver flower centers.

Other bias tubes encircle the waist and button in place. This also gives a more finished look. As a whole, such details are not found in the pattern. These are extras you add that elevate the quality of the entire garment. I absorb many of these little tips while looking at pricey ready-to-wear. Quick and easy is fine if you need an instant wardrobe. At this point in my life, I only want to do things that are truly elegant and worthy of the investment of my time.

Where did the jacket lower shaped band come from? It's the top several inches of a Bonfit skirt patterner or the lower edge of the bodice patterner. The jacket is only cut down to the waistline plus 1" for a seam and slight blousing. The skirt patterner is traced off on paper, then seam

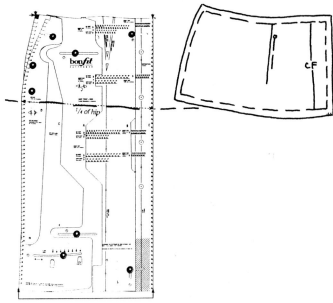

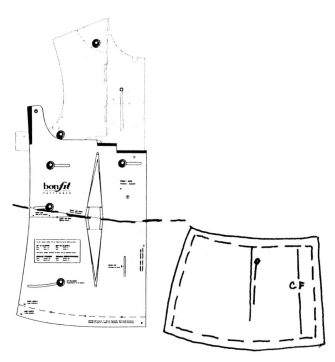

This can take some time to sew all the way around the appliqué edges, but what a lovely way for a work of art to be reborn. I have the advantage of travelling and finding treasures such as these kimono panels. If you like the look, can you create something similar on your own? Yes, if your machine has the embroidery capability. One of my memory cards has a very similar flower. I've previously done something like that in silver on a black lapel that will snap on a suit. Remember at the end of series 12 we did a lot of lapels and dickeys like this. They're great wardrobe expanders.

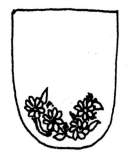

allowances are added. Add an overlap at the center front for buttons and buttonholes. Pin out the dart because it will be better and flatter in the hip area without it. This will force the waistline to curve upward at the side seams. It rounds around the body now very nicely. This area will be interfaced completely with a suit-weight woven fusible. The band backing layer may be either more fashion fabric or a lining fabric layer.

Another good project for this type of embroidery would be the platter purses from series 8 (clutch bags). Embroider the oval, then fuse on a backing and make a beautiful evening bag. A later chapter in this book gives more ideas.

The recycled wedding kimono is only part of the "celebration in pink" this program features. There's another very joyous celebration going on - the celebration of life.

See Photo 1401 Page 13

At the Houston Quilt Festival, I met this wonderfully talented lady. JoAnn Musso from Dallas is her name and back on series 13 you saw a lovely ruby red outfit of hers with Dior roses on it. Here is another of her creations - a beautiful pink crepe suit she has named "Celebration in Pink". JoAnn is celebrating the fifth anniversary of her breast surgery. That is indeed a reason to rejoice - she's passed her fifth anniversary - now closer to six years. Not only is JoAnn grateful, but she has a message for every one of you. Early detection is all important to catch breast cancer in its earliest stage. A regular mammogram will detect irregularities before anything else. Please, get a mammogram now.

JoAnn's whole jacket has been channel quilted with silver thread. When choosing metallic thread types, think of the end use. If embroidering, you can use either twisted thread or the flat sliced glitzy type. You must decide to have a soft patina or a super shiny sparkle - either will work. This is a personal preference - you might even need to try a little of each to decide. When quilting it might be better to use the stronger twisted thread to make sure there's no breakage. Also, it's a good idea to use one of the special needles made for metallic thread. These have a larger eye and the thread has much less friction as it passes through the needle. JoAnn also embroidered and beaded

within the rattail loops on the shoulders. The rayon rattail cord comes in a wide variety of colors, and is nice to couch into designs or use as an edging, couching it in place.

Yo-Yos start out as larger circles of fabric. A gathering stitch all around the edge is then drawn up to the center and the finished circle will be half its original cut size.

The final touch on this lovely celebration jacket is the Dior roses. They begin as football-shaped fabric cutouts. Fold over in half, the raw edge on bottom, fold on top. Stitch a gathering stitch around the raw edges, holding them together, and draw up that thread slightly. Roll up sideways, securing the bottom with a couple of stitches. Wrap two more petals around this alternating opening.

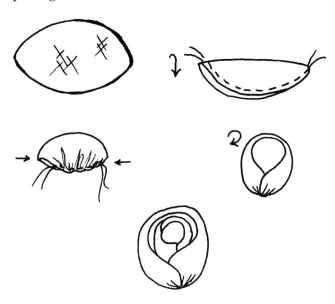

That's what happened in Houston, and we're going to travel a lot of places this series. Everywhere I go something triggers a sewing idea and I never know what the next adventure will be. Come along with me next time and we'll see what happens in another great city!

Questions? Breast Cancer Hotline:
1-800-IM-AWARE (1-800-462-9273)

Ease-Y   Chapter 2

If you are very young, you are possibly still trying to find out who you are — what feels right to you. At my age I know. Quick and easy is simply not my style. I only want the best and that's why I sew. I can have the best fabrics in my preferred colors with the most perfectly coordinated notions and buttons. I can have the finest detailing, all exquisitely finished and fitted to my personal bumps, bulges and figure flukes — and in my price range. When you sew you call the shots and can have it all. Don't you love it!

Then why is this program called Ease-Y? It's because it will all deal with ease. Where do you add ease for different types of garments and in what amounts? How is this affected by fashion's whim? We are moving out of an era of over-sized garments. Things are now being pared down somewhat but there is a strong element of choice. Let personal preferences lead the way. Many garments are body-conscious but if the form-fitting thing is not for you, go the classic route, and your garment will last much longer. Always have an eye for what is honestly most flattering on you, not what looks good on that fashion model.

As you've probably realized through the years, the majority of my wardrobe begins as a basic pattern and from that anything else can be designed. If you change size how often do you have to buy new basic patterns? As fashion's foibles flip-flop how often will that also demand new purchases?

The obvious solution is to begin with an adjustable patterner and never buy another. Bonfit America has these in bodice, skirt and pant units and any style can be made from these plastic sturdy adjustable basics. Put on a few pounds this year? That's OK. Loosen the patterner knobs and enlarge it to your exact dimensions. If you lose some, adjust it smaller and the same patterner keeps on working for your newest specifications.

I have a friend who doesn't sew but wears a size 10 no matter what size she actually is. She shops endlessly, trying on clothes in every brand. When she finds a size 10 she can get into, she'll

buy it!! The nice thing about the Bonfit is there isn't a size on it, so no such mere number need concern you. Adjust it to your actual measurements and it will fit every time.

This is the starting point - taking measurements. There is a measuring chart in the book that comes with each unit. All the areas pertinent to that type of garment are listed on the chart. The bodice patterner has 14 measurement blanks but for most garments not all those measurements will be used. The skirt, a simple garment, has 4 and there are 8 for pants.

Be sure to take these measurements in the undergarments you would wear under the clothing article you are making. This means for a blouse, measure over a bra. But if this will be a jacket you wear over a sweater, measure yourself with the sweater on. Isn't this sensible? Isn't this logical? - and that's exactly what designing your own clothing is - very logical with this adjustable patterner.

To get comfortable with the patterner's usage, of course, watch the accompanying video first. To see it being used answers any questions you may have and explains usage very quickly. The first time I used it my main concern was in the matter of ease. Would there be enough to actually make the garment wearable, or for fitting purposes, would it be like the checked gingham bodices we used to make from commercial paper patterns? They did indeed fit the body when altered and adjusted at great length. But they most assuredly were too tight to make up in nice fabric for a wearable garment!

See Photo 1402 Page 13

The taupe blouse in this photo was made from the patterner with the ease built into it. The fabric is a rather heavy silk charmeuse. The floating front panel is a duplicate of the blouse front with the right shoulder cut wider to pleat before stitching into the shoulder seam. The lower layer edge curves downward from the right shoulder edge to the left side seam at waist level. Because of the fabric weight and the extra layer, its size should not be excessive. I was thrilled to see how perfectly this worked out from the Bonfit, no fitting changes made.

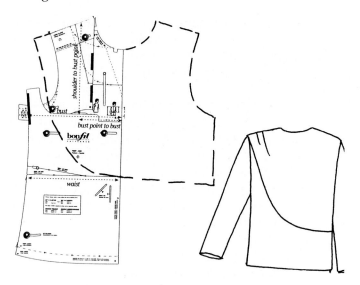

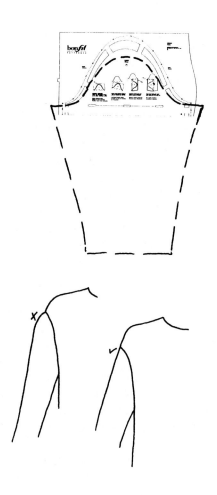

Another blouse in this series is an aqua silk in program 1410. This was a thinner fabric and the thinner the fabric, the larger the garment must be to look graceful. I moved its side out 1" which widened the shoulder making it drop over the edge of the shoulder point 1". This also made the bust and hip measurement larger by 4" (the patterner is only 1/4 the total blouse). When a garment has dropped shoulders, the same amount added to the bodice is removed from the sleeve cap. This is so that where bodice and sleeve cap meet the line will be smooth, not puffed out awkwardly. Of course when this cap is flattened 1" it measures less across the top. Add 1" to each side and it will measure the same as the armscye of the bodice. Remember in dropped shoulders there will be no fullness, no easing of the sleeve cap because again you want smoothness, not puffiness. If you want to drop this line very far you have the option of removing the sleeve panel shoulder replacing it with the cut-on sleeve template.

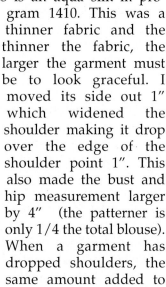

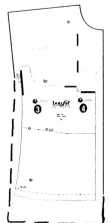

That was what happened to the purple pant top seen under the pin-woven vest in program 1405. The original unit was a little shaped on the side seams. Probably you would straighten that line as you add ease.

My next adventure was making a sleeveless shell to wear under a suit. For this, I used the Bonfit as is, with the bust dart on the lower front panel, no ease added or subtracted. The only change is cutting out the neckline and armscye somewhat. Remarkable how you can truly make any top you desire!

Through the years you've noticed I make a lot of jackets. Can even these be made from this bodice patterner? Certainly - but probably you'll want more ease to allow for wearing over blouses

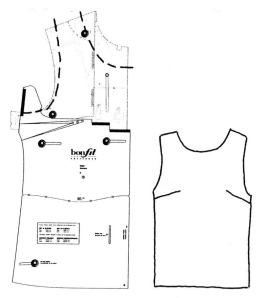

dresses or sweaters. I set the patterner 1 1/2" on the bust measurements beyond my actual measurement. This adds the extra ease all over including more needed for interfacing and lining. It extends the shoulders slightly but if you plan shoulder pads slope a little more height out at the sleeve edge of the bodice shoulder. Also suit sleeves need to hang straighter so choose the top line on the tem-

plate for a high standard sleeve cap, add a little more still for the shoulder pad. This will measure more than the bodice armscye because some cap ease will be worked in.

With experience comes the assurance that this works, and you can design anything you want from a basic pattern. In early beginnings it would be wise to go through your closet to find garments similar to what you want to make. Compare these measurements with a basic to add or subtract a little ease. Keep remembering the amount of ease not only on fashion's whim, but also the type of garment and the weight of the fabric to be used.

Your designs can be traced directly on fabric from a patterner, adding seam allowances. I usually draw this on fabric with a chalk wheel which later easily brushes off. This is when I plan to make the garment once.

If the garment will be made repeatedly, I'll draw it on pattern tracer and add all seams to it. The type with a printed grid always indicates the straight grain. It can be purchased off the bolt in a fabric shop's interfacing department.

I've made two of these for suit jackets, a big one and a little jacket. I've made over 50 variations by now of that little fitted jacket and have several more imagined for the future. This comes from using the lower bodice panel with the waist dart. If you look at photos in any of the 13 Sewing Connection books preceding this one, you'll see many variations of this with necklines changed from high to V to any shape imaginable. Some

overlap in front to button, others only touch at center front for a bolero type. Some are long, covering the hip area, others are cut off nearer the waist. A third possibility in this area is to have a hip band sewn on as in the pink suit of program 1401 on the book cover. A Celebration of Jackets is a 90 minute video I did to show how simply these

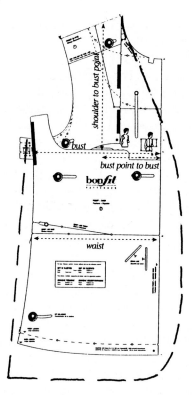

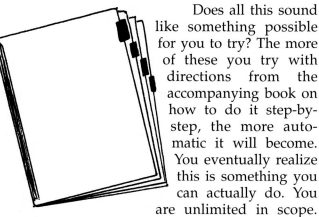

Does all this sound like something possible for you to try? The more of these you try with directions from the accompanying book on how to do it step-by-step, the more automatic it will become. You eventually realize this is something you can actually do. You are unlimited in scope. Whatever you see, whatever you imagine, you can have. I'm convinced that yes, you too can do this!

changes can be made from a basic.

The big jacket is similar but I've made the sleeve less fitted with a wider wrist for a more casual, generous cut. The neckline I usually cut in a V style, but it can work cutting the bodice of the jacket in one piece. This will work when the fabric is a little wider than your body circumference.

How do you store these basic patterns once you have them made? One way is to create a storage book. From an art or office supply or even a grocery store, buy several sheets of poster board. All these I tape together with wide celophane or duct tape. Little tabs on each open edge identify the contents. Mine are categorized into big jacket, little jacket, blouse, T-shirt, vest, bodice shell, pants and skirt.

Anyone compartment contains all the pieces for that particular pattern, all clearly labeled. To make sure at a later date I remember what the pattern was used for, I might pin to it little swatches of fabric from the various projects made. Then I can go to a closet, find the garment and try it on to see if this is the fit I want for the new project I'll make. This "book" is easily stored under a couch in my sewing room or wherever it will stay safely flat, without wrinkling or folding the pattern pieces.

1401 – JoAnn Musso's beautiful pink crepe suit she has named "Celebration in Pink".

Displaying jacket pictured on front cover, made with the Bonfit Patterner.

1402 – Scraps from these garments went into pillow and vest. See Chapter 4.

Prime Cuts Chapter 3

Over the past several years the rotary cutter has been a wonderful aid for cutting straight lines quickly and uniformly. Good things just got better. For some pin weaving projects, I needed to cut many bias strips in a whole variety of different widths. To make every cut you must lift the ruler to move it to the next location. This isn't a problem in many fabrics, especially if they are short lengths, to cut one at a time or several stacked. A real problem occurs when you cut really long strips, with the fabric folded several times. This can be compounded when dealing with a fabric which is extremely slippery and which moves around every time you lift the ruler. Further complications can occur when you have very springy fabric which not only slides, but pops up every time pressure is released.

Enter a new product! Strips Ahoy has come on the scene to solve these problems. Three cheers for a marvellous innovation! Where can you get it? Directly from the company - address and phone number at the end of this chapter. You can check in your local area for outlets like quilt, fabric or craft shops. Give them the Coming Attractions number and tell them The Sewing Connection sent you.

What is this new wonder? It's a combination cutting mat and slotted template. It hinges by screws at the top (which can be removed, but no need to!). The slotted template lifts up to arrange your fabric underneath, then is lowered to hold it all in place while you cut multiple strips without having to move anything. The slotted area is 18" wide with slots every 1/2", or 36 slots. These are 13" long and just wide enough to run your rotary blade through, which makes for a nice clean cut every time. The inches are marked in both directions, with the markings on top of your fabric rather than underneath like other cutting mats. There is also a big X on top to mark a 45° angle.

Chapter 3

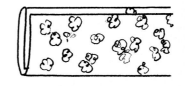

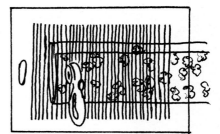

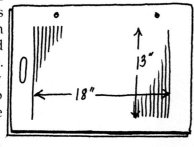

To cut strips for piecing and quilting, you fold your fabric pieces on the straight, so that they are narrower top to bottom than the 13". Think how accurately and quickly you can strip a yard of fabric when you don't have to use a ruler after every cut.

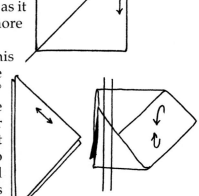

If you are making tubes of fabric, bindings or welting, you might want to cut the fabric on the bias, as it will then lie more softly and smoothly. This means you cut the fabric on a 45° angle. Align the bias cuts together and fold that diagonal line so the upper and lower corners overlap in the center. Fold again if necessary, until the fabric is less than 13" from top to bottom.

Arrange the folded fabric under the slotted plate and lower it down to hold the fabric. You will have to apply some pressure with your free hand as you progress cutting strips. You can cut all fabric under the 18" width without moving anything on the Strips Ahoy. There is also an anchor plate to hold in your other hand which is pressing down the template.

Now there's the matter of deciding on widths for each strip. I wanted both wide and narrow tubes of every fabric used. Remember, in tubes you will have the top and bottom layers, plus two 1/4" seam allowances. Add these together to determine how wide the strips need to be. My narrowest tubes are 1/2", which means the fabric strip will be 1 1/2" wide. This would be 3 slots over, since they are each 1/2" apart. The widest tube is a little over 2", so that strip would be 5" wide, or 10 slots over. Several of my tubes were various widths in between. How much quicker this is than to cut, cut, cut.

When finished, lift your Strips Ahoy by the big slotted handle at one end. The Strips Ahoy stores flat or can be hung on a wall or in a cabinet. Before putting it away, let's think what else it can be used for.

Think of decorating a polar fleece jacket with giant "rickrack" of man-made suede or leather. This would be easier to stitch on if its first fused in place. Accordion fold a strip of one of the fusibles with a peel-off paper. Experiment first with any sheet of paper to decide how far apart the folds will be.

Line up the folded edges with the 45° mark. Decide how wide this should be, and cut 2 pieces. Open up the rickrack. Its ready to fuse on the leather backside. You can see plainly to cut out at the fusible edges. If the fabric is very thin it can be folded and cut directly. Most fabric this thin is also ravelly and not suitable for this idea. Non-wovens whose edges won't ravel are generally too thick to cut through the many layers, so they would produce only a very short strip.

Series 9 of *The Sewing Connection* featured a program on scrap baskets. This took endless strips 1 1/2" wide, cut on the straight or cross grain. Think how quickly these pieces can now be cut

up, without having to move a ruler, using a quick Fiskars rotary cutter rolled through every third slot. When you have a few minutes here or there to do a little work, prepare and keep a roll of these handy. After cutting there is no need for the strips to be joined. The loose ends merely overlap as the strips are wound around a core welting before zigzagging them together into a basket shape.

In Series 3, we presented a coat with a big shaggy collar, which remains as popular 11 series later!! It is made of polar fleece, which is a really hot item now. One terrific feature of these fleeces, as well as suedes, is that raw edges don't ravel, which make them perfect fringes. At that time I painstakingly cut all those slashes with scissors, which took forever to get them all uniformly slashed. The same was true for a little bog coat in Series 12 - made before Strips Ahoy was on the market. Just think how easy these shawl collars will be with the slotted wonder!

When fringing any long edge, fold sideways, which allows for several layers to be cut at once. Slide them under the template as far as you need to get the right length slashes. The area of fabric below the Strips Ahoy will remain unslashed.

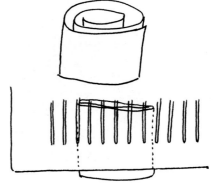

The lines are marked in the clear plastic on top of your fabric, which allows you to see exactly what you are doing. Roll the Fiskars cutters quick as a wink

1403a – Beautiful silk vest and cumerbund with hundreds of tiny pieces stitched together, by Priscilla Kibbee.

1403b – Here is a black cotton vest echoing repetitive cuts by Maria Montgomery.

1403c & d – Cathy Carroll created "Simba" using untold layers of fabric all cut in fringes.

1403e & f – These buffalos are made with suede bodies topped with yarn needle-punched all over head and shoulders, by Martha Richards.

through every slot and the multi-layers are perfectly, uniformly cut. It's a dream come true - one minute as opposed to over an hour.

Another possibility is an interior fringe connected solidly at either side. If a piece of fabric is folded over, with cuts made across the fold, this opens up several ideas. The one I'll use is for a clutch bag made of Ultra Suede. Stitch a different color fabric under the slashed area. Stitch down the center of the slashes, turning each one over with tweezers when you come to it. At each slash the underlying color will show through. If you want these 1/4" slashes rather than 1/2", after slashing the whole length, carefully move it halfway so the cuts are centered between the slots. Slash again, and you'll have 1/4" cuts.

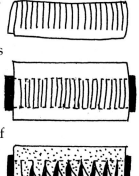

See Photo 1403a Page 16

Priscilla Kibbee of Wolcott, New York, made a really beautiful silk vest and cummerbund with hundreds of tiny pieces stitched together on the straight, on the diagonal, in squares and stripes. The pieces are in the most luscious shades of several rich turquoise fabrics with little touches of purple. The jewel colors fairly vibrate as they play off each other. This was made a little while ago, before the Strips Ahoy was on the market. What a wonderful help it would have been! You can see from the photo what small pieces are involved in these several variations of Seminole piecing.

Initially she could have cut all her long 15" widths really quickly, every other slot. By the time 1/4" seams were stitched, 1/2" strips would remain. These were cut across to do the second phase of piecing, with the fascinating joinings done to make this complicated design.

See Photo 1403b Page 16

Maria Montgomery of Victoria, British Columbia, made a pretty vest, echoing repetitive cuts. Hers is black cotton, all cut in 1 1/2" straight grain strips. This is a stitch and flip quilt-as-you-go technique. After a strip is flipped up, some prairie points are laid on the strip,

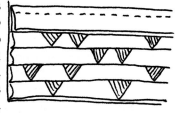

with the raw top edges aligned. Another strip covers the first, then stitched and flipped up. You start at the bottom and stitch all this to a fabric backing.

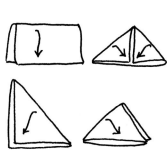

The prairie points are squares about 1 1/2" that can be folded on the straight or on the diagonal as you prefer. When folded, either press, or hold together temporarily with a little dab of glue.

See Photo 1403c & 1403d Page 16

Cathy Carroll of Wichita, Kansas, certainly did a lot of cutting on her "Simba" coat - untold layers of fabric all cut in fringes. What a blessing Strips Ahoy is for cutting such a large amount, saving all sorts of tedious work. These are all 1/2" cuts on her garment, cut on bias strips, 4" wide. After cutting, these rows began at the top of the jacket to stitch on the base fabric upside down.  Each successive row is attached about 1/2" lower. When the sewing is complete, a shake of the jacket makes all the fringe slip over to hang down with added loft - rather like backcombing your hair. This cutting can be done in a flash by having the lower edge of the fabric layers protected again by the unslotted Strips Ahoy framework.

See Photo 1403e & 1403f Page 16

Martha Richards of Garland, Texas, designed this wonderful buffalo coat, inspired by the birth last year of a white buffalo in Wisconsin. These buffalo are made with suede bodies topped with

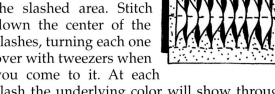

yarn needle-punched all over head and shoulders. Lots of little beads glisten in the fur and curved beads look exactly like buffalo horns. It's title is "If you've seen one buffalo you seen 'em all." I love the humor of these gifted fiber artists. The southwest influence is alive here, so long suede fringe is a natural. Can you imagine cutting this all 6" long and 1/4" wide, or even narrower? The Strips Ahoy is a perfect tool for this, and here's how.

Remember, the slotted area is 13" long. Because a rotary cutter is round it cannot cut to the ends of the slot, but will leave about 1/2" top and bottom uncut. Remember also I said this remarkable tool is a cutting board bolted to the slotted guide on top. What is screwed together can be easily unscrewed.

Cut your suede piece the 18" X 13" size of the slotted area. Remove the Strips Ahoy screws so you now have two separate pieces. Position the suede on the lower board. Line up the slotted cover on top. With your rotary cutter, cut through every slot top to bottom with your Fiskars rotary cutter. That 1/2" top and bottom remains intact. Then carefully lift the slotted cover, move it sideways 1/4" and repeat cutting it all. If the suede is thin enough, do all this with it folded in half lengthwise or crosswise.

Lastly, move the cover edge down to the halfway point, so its long edge is in the center of the suede. One cut across horizontally and you now have two rows of that long narrow fringe perfectly cut.

June Greig is a sewing friend from St. Louis who does magnificent work and teaches her techniques. You'll see several of June's creations crop up throughout this series to provide you with wonderful inspiration. Where was she inspired? She worked for years at one of the nation's top retailers and you can see the influences of Missoni, Geoffrey Beene, and many other world renowned designers in her work later on.

This knit top has an exterior facing cut in two layers hanging extra long. The fringe is cut on the lengthwise direction, pulled and it curls to the backside, then the ends are tied in knots. That fringe is about 7" long, 1/2" wide.

As I so frequently tell you, it's possible to do whatever you want. "You can do it", and doubly so when you have the right equipment! As a sewer, I'm already wondering how I got along without Strips Ahoy. If you're a quilter multiply that thought as you'd use it constantly.

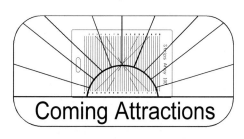

Look for Strips Ahoy™ 100 and Companion Products in your local quilt shop or sewing store. If unavailable, you can order by contacting:

Coming Attractions
3104 E Camelback Road, Suite 213
Phoenix, AZ 85016
Phone: (602) 468-1938
Fax: (602) 954-8772

Tubular Treasures   *Chapter 4*

Fabric tubes are indispensable on garments shown throughout this series. They're wonderful as buttonloops or ties in belts and fastenings. Curved around in various places they might provide a transition between two different fabrics as they cover the joining seams. Small tubes might have large-holed beads strung on them for accents. All these little touches have the look of caring, of attention to detail, of completeness.

A great abundance of these tubes can be carried a step beyond the accent stage. They can be used to actually become the garment. This is a marvelous way to coordinate wardrobe items, using tubes of leftover fabric from several, weaving them together to build a new fabric. Not only do the colors play off each other in a lively way, but also a combination of textures from shiny to matte, from smooth to pebbly makes an interesting whole. The examples shown in this program are a vest and a pillow because the same fabrics can be used for fashion as well as home decor.

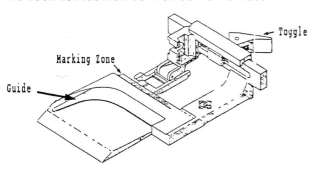

While we're mass producing, let's also stitch bias tubes for another program. The whole range of fabrics being sewn right now include suede cloth, wool gauze, silk charmeuse, microfiber, upholstery fabric, organza, chiffon, and brocade. With this conglomeration of difficult to control fabrics, a Fastube Foot is very reassuring. The fabric folds over the guide and a perfectly uniform tube is stitched every time. The toggle opens to adjust it wider or narrower and whatever the fabric, there are no more worries about lack of uniformity. The right equipment makes an incredible difference.

Whatever the size and whatever the fabric, the Crowning Touch people have provided a tube

turner which will do the job. A whole array of brass tubes in graduated sizes are available to turn fabric tubes up to the size of your thumb. Beyond this a new line has been added in plastic to accommodate still larger diameters and heavier fabrics.

The ingenious simplicity of these Fasturns allows for successfully turning the fabric right-side-out because the fabric surfaces never touch each other. After stitching, the smooth tube is inserted in one end of the fabric tube and the fabric is all crushed down until it is completely on the Fasturn. Through the hollow tube center insert the turner, a long wire with a handle on one end, a "corkscrew" on the other. Screw it into the fabric tip at the far end where it is extending slightly past the Fasturn opening. Then pull the wire handle and fabric through the tube center while pushing the unturned fabric up on the outside of the tube with your other hand. Because the smooth tube is always between the two fabric surfaces, there is no resistance to layers of fabric rubbing against themselves. Even corduroy and upholstery fabrics are possible to turn over the large size tubes.

Another lovely feature is that as the fabric is pulled to the inside over the edge of the tube, the seam allowances automatically open (once you start it that way). They then get somewhat pressed open much like finger pressing would do. It is also possible to cord the fabric tube by putting the cord or welting end up to touch the fabric as it is being turned. It automatically gets pulled into the inside of the fabric tube.

These two projects will not be corded. Instead they will be pressed flat once turned. If this final usage is reversible, press so the seam is on the flat edge. If only one side will show it doesn't matter if the seam is there or if only on the back side of each tube. Now let's make some good use of these pressed tubes.

Woven Pillow of Tubes and Ribbon

This will be a pillow 14" square finished size, but 15" before sewing. The weaving will be done on a padded board covered by a fabric grid which will later allow pressing. You need the straight lines vertically and horizontally to aid you in positioning fabric tubes. Any checked or plaid fabric would do the job.

The fabric tubes chosen for this perfectly coordinate with the colors of the furniture upholstery on which the pillow will be used. This is a mixture of fabric textures for pleasing combinations. There are also velvet and organdy ribbons in this to introduce another color as well as interesting variety. These are actually fashion fabrics of silk charmeuse, some used on the satin side, others on the matte side which also produces slightly different color gradations. Another fabric tube is a suede cloth and that same fashsion fabric is used for the outer edge welting and the solid pillow back. Fashion fabrics can be used in the home just as some upholstery and drapery fabrics can be used for clothing.

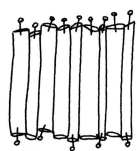

A 15" square on the board grid is covered by tubes, all laid lengthwise touching each other side by side. Vary the colors, widths, and textures irregularly until you like the arrangement. Pin the top of every tube to the pad, slanting the pin heads outward rather flat. At the bottom pin every other one, leaving the in between ones free.

Now flip upward all those whose bottom edges are free. Lay across these a selection of more tubes and ribbons, again rearranging until you like the effect. Leave a space between each horizonal as alternate strips will be woven in later.

Bring down all the vertical tubes which have been slipped up, to lay across the horizonal tubes. The verticals have filled the whole space touching each other

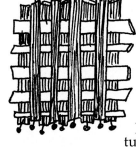

unlike the horizontals which leave spaces between each. Pin down the bottom ends of the loose vertical tubes.

Using a bodkin, some clamp tweezers, or whatever slender gripping device you have, clamp it to a new tube end and begin weaving it horizontally through the remaining spaces until everything is filled. Readjust where necessary to get all strips straight. Also pin all the horizontal ends when it is solidly woven.

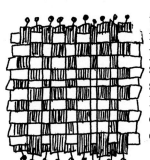

Cut a 15" square of thin fusible interfacing. Position it on top of your woven project, fusible side down. Press it with a steam iron to fuse it in place. Remove all pins and fuse completely on all these edges.

Interfacing side up, staystitch outer edge of the square about 1/4" from the outside. Trim off any tubes which extend past the interfacing. On the right side (woven side up) of the square the welting will be applied.

See Photo 1404a Page 25

If during this you flashed a thought that big bias tape rather than tubes would have taken less fabric, you are correct. From the start you must decide if fabric economy is the first priority. For me it was not. To see a pillow like this up close, tells you that sheer luxury is the primary goal. The soft luster of a fashion silk used as an accessory for the home is recognizable quality. We're not looking at a pillow found in the discount home shops for $15. Add another zero to this, because you'll find similar items in designer home shops for $150 and up. These items I won't buy, but I love to look them over. To feel the essence of top quality and duplicate it in my sewing room is a wonderful reason to sew.

Vest Pattern from Bonfit

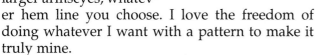

Any garment can be made from a Bonfit patterner and it's certainly simple to change the bodice patterner into a vest. Loosen the knobs and move the units apart until your measurements register on the indicators. Tighten the knobs. From this line drawing of the patterner the dotted lines show how you would actually cut out this vest, adding seams but cutting a V neckline and larger armscyes, whatever hem line you choose. I love the freedom of doing whatever I want with a pattern to make it truly mine.

Tubular Vests

Any size tube will be usable in this vest from 2" at the corners to 15" in the longest expanses. That is because the 26" X 12" rectangle being woven is on the bias. The pillow and the vest were made using leftover fabric pieces but there was no need to sew together the strips to make them longer for they would then only need to be cut down. Rather, all the bias strips made into tubes would be fine somewhere, whatever the length.

The same taupe tubes leftover from the pillow will be used in the vest, eliminating all the navy ribbons. Since taupe is possibly not my best color, bright pink tubes and ribbons will be good color additions for the vest. To have several projects like this going on at once means better use of my time, mass producing wherever possible.

The same grid covered board used for the pillow will be used to weave the vest. There is a 45° angle marked on it which makes it quite simple to lay your fabric tubes on the diagonal.

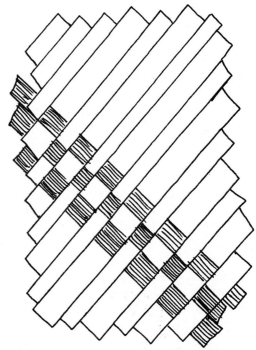

Line up the first couple of tubes in each direction with this X and the rest fall into line. Cover the rectangular space with a variety of color, texture, width of the tubes all going one direction. Pin all ends to the board, slanting pinheads outward.

Then use a bodkin, clamp tweezers or other device to help you to weave another set of tubes the opposite direction. When the weaving is finished way out to the corners, cover with a thin fusible interfacing cut to size and fuse. Same as with the pillow, staystitch the edges and trim off excess tubes.

Now decide exactly what you'll do with this diagonally woven panel. I cut my panel in two pieces, like this sketched plan, after first drawing

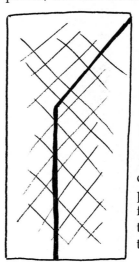

the cutting line and staystitching on each side of it. The narrower piece with its wing on top became the left center front, that wing angling out to the shoulder. The wider, shorter piece was turned upside down and used on the vest right front, the slant end defining the vest's single pocket. The rest of the vest front uses larger pieces of the same fabrics comprising the tubes, piecing as space demands. Extra bias strips cut but not used form piping around all edges.

The joy of this fun type sewing is that it evolves along the way. Rarely do I know at the outset how the finished product will look - exactly. It's like reading a mystery novel you just can't put down. You have to read to the end to see how it all turns out.

What will the rest of the vest be to balance those heavy woven panels? The best alternative seemed to be quilting it to a cotton flannel. My New Home Memorycraft 9000 has a built-in butterfly along with many other quilting designs. A few of these on the back can be automatically stitched first, then surround them with a meadow of long wavy grasses of stitched lines. This is not only decorative, but it holds the layers in place. Finish the back off with a belt to give the waist some definition.

See Photo 1404b Page 25

Could you do all this on a dress or a jacket without overwhelming yourself as well as the whole outfit? Doubtful. Everyone has a personal flamboyance factor. The larger the project, the more courage will be required to carry it off. A vest is a wonderful little garment, great on which to indulge your fantasy sewing in a small area. Tone it down then by wearing it over a more reserved pant or skirted outfit.

The use of a Fastube foot to uniformly stitch the tubes and the set of Fasturns to turn them right-side out make these very pleasant activities. These well-engineered products are found in most fabric, quilting and sewing machine shops. If unable to find them locally, write to:

Pin Weaving

In recent years, and with good reason, we've all seen several ways of pin weaving. To weave on a loom you must have a big loom and a studio large enough to house it or them (if several). We can't all do that. Pin weaving can be done on a small scale, and is something everyone can do.

Instead of weaving big long pieces of fabric, then cutting out a garment to construct - this involves weaving only the small shaped parts needed. These might be collars or pockets or yokes, or something as big as a vest front, but rarely larger.

Your weaving materials might be yarns and cords throughout, or in combination with wider ribbons. Sometimes strips of fabric are used or even fabric tubes. In the last chapter the weaving was only fabric tubes and ribbons woven in both directions. Now we will use tubes as the crosswise or filling, but the "loom" will be warped, with cords strung lengthwise.

In the diagram you see pins all stuck in a padded board in the shape of a vest front. The lengthwise cord is all strung between the pins and a little weaving has begun. Any source I've seen seems to begin this way, but my mind moved ahead at this point. The question is how to remove pins upon completion without it falling apart. Great effort down the tube! Back to square one, let's think through what would work successfully. Without a fusible backing this project seemed doomed. So I pulled out the pins and made a fresh start.

The pattern started as the Bonfit basic. Notice by the dotted line the armscye has been made larger. The neck is brought down to a V and a little extra ease is added at the side seams. The vest fronts are in points at the lower edges. The Bonfit

patterner can be positioned directly on the fabric to mark around the edges before cutting it out. If it seems likely a pattern or a certain style will be used several times, it makes sense to figure this out only once as you cut it out in grid-marked pattern tracers to save for the next time. Memory is short, and when you need to use this procedure another time you need to recall what it was. The swatch reminds you and then it would be wise to try on the garment made previously to be sure it is just right for the new clothing.

From this pattern, I cut out in a fusible interfacing the same shape, but 1" larger all the way around. A little leeway when cutting out is good insurance, as the pin woven fabric could shrink when the pins are not holding it taut.

Position this fusible shape on a padded surface, fusible side up. That padded board is manufactured commercially and can be purchased. It can also be improvised. Here's how - pad a thin piece of plywood or even stiff heavy cardboard. Use some checked fabric as a top cover to provide a set of straight lines in both directions 1/4" or 1/2" apart. Secure on the backside and this is ready to go.

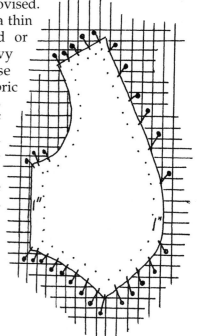

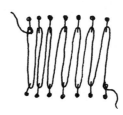
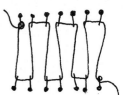

The pins I chose are not my usual beloved 1 1/4" glass head fine pins - .05mm in diameter. These are heavy duty pins about .06mm, because sturdy holders seemed desirable for this job. In retrospect it probably wouldn't have mattered much. Use whatever you have.

All the pins are stuck in a rather flat fashion, heads leaning away from the project. These should be about 1/4" apart. The grid or checked fabric in the background enables you to achieve this uniformity. These pins only need to be top and bottom as the cords will be strung vertically. This cord can be pointed at each end if you want them closer together when weaving yarns or narrow ribbons. I wanted mine further apart for wide fabric tubes, so I squared off each end over two pins.

The cord used can be anything strong enough for the job, like pearl cotton, heavy decorative threads, ribbon floss, strong yarns, etc. Start out by stringing it over just a few pins and weaving a few rows of the intended filling to see if it looks like you planned. I started with a ribbon floss, but decided it was too slippery (the fabric tubes kept spreading out wider), and it was too visible. A trial or practice is always a good idea.

From the last program, Tubular Treasures, the filmy chiffon and organza bias-cut fabric tubes had already been mass produced. Now, its only a matter of weaving them over and under the vertical cords.

I used five different fabrics in this vest. Longer or shorter fabric tubes can all be used somewhere, so don't bother to join them into long pieces. These also varied in diameter from 1/2" up to 1 1/2". These were randomly woven, mixing up the sizes and fabrics. A clamping tool of some sort makes this job easier. A bodkin would be a good choice; I used some clamping tweezers. These held the end of the tube in their clamp,

handle first, while the smooth metal easily pulled the tube over and under. Some of the short tubes don't go all the way across, but end wherever the tube end occurs. Some were squished here, spread out there to purposely make the rows irregular. Undulating waves of this thin soft fabric appealed to me more than the usual perfect rows stiffly and evenly woven.

When all the fusible interfacing vest shape is covered with the weaving, set it permanently in place. Cover the whole area with a press cloth and steam press, fusing the weaving to the backing. Give it a minute to cool and dry out, then carefully pull out all the straight pins. Much to my delight nothing moved, I had expected the woven piece to compress to something smaller, but nothing happened. With the interfacing on top, turn the piece over and fuse again.

Position the pattern on top and cut the edges to size, then treat it as any other piece of fabric when constructing the garment. The fusible backing holds it secure, but this particular piece would have been impossible without the security of the backing. Also those tubes squished together work only because the fabrics are very thin and supple. Heavier fabrics would make this seem more like a rug than a piece of fabric. It's possibly also a good idea to do rows of a wavy stitch of monofilament thread all over the pinwoven fabric before making up the garment. It won't show but will guarantee that you won't have to repair any slippage at a later date.

Your whole garment could be pin woven. I decided the right front was enough and chose to make the left front and back of something else. A raw silk with a print in similar colors is heavy enough to balance the woven side. This is backed by fusible interfacing to beef it up a little. A second reason is silk ravels terribly and the fusible glues all the edge yarns safely, securely together. This is covered by one of the filmy transparent chiffons used for tubes in the woven front.

Rather than just covering the raw silk the chiffon is all textured, and wrinkled across the surface. My first idea for these wrinkles held permanently in place was to wind fusible thread on the bobbin. On the long stitches setting, stitch curvy random lines on your base fabric, upside down, so the fusible thread is on the raw silk side,

1404a – To see a pillow up close, tells you that sheer luxury is the primary goal.

1404b – Tubes and ribbons created the vest.

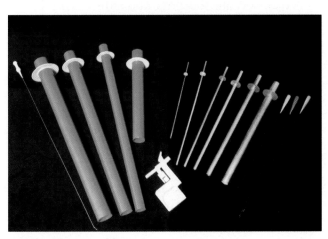

1404 – Fasturn Show

1405 – Grace France's pin woven jacket, not surprisingly, has won a couple of prestigious shows.

The Memorycraft 9000 – child's play. A 3 year old can do it!.

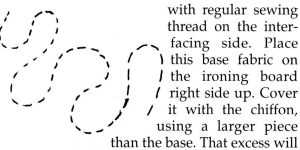

with regular sewing thread on the interfacing side. Place this base fabric on the ironing board right side up. Cover it with the chiffon, using a larger piece than the base. That excess will be needed when you produce wrinkles. With your fingers, distribute this excess fabric evenly, then fuse, flattening it in place, with a steam iron.

I always like to experiment first on this , using a scrap before proceeding to the actual garment. No ripping, no redoing, which saves time in the long run.

What had seemed like an obvious success was not. The chiffon pulled loose from the fusible thread much too easily. Something more permanent was required to secure the wrinkles in place.

A new product, which proved to be a viable solution, is now available from Coats and Clark. Instant Seam is a double-faced sticky transparent tape with a peel-off backing. It is also labelled Instant Hem and Instant Stick and Hold on various convenient packaging. These are all the same product and are packaged in 1/4" and 1/2" wide rolls It is also packaged in Instant Stick and Hold sheets for use in appliquéing. There is a peel-off sheet on both sides so it can be peeled, stuck to the fabric, and cut out for the appliqué. Peel off the other side and position the appliqué on another fabric surface. This sticky backing temporarily holds and can be repositioned should you change your mind. If you want it to become permanent, press, and it is fused forever. It is washable. Don't

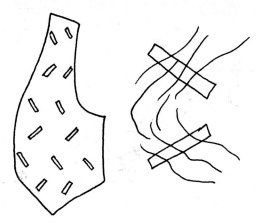

satin stitch the edges, as it's not a good idea to stitch through this. Merely fuse it and leave it alone. Notice when shopping - there are two distinct varieties of Stick and Hold - one for fabrics, and one for crafts. So observe that distinction (on the package top corner).

I cut 1 1/2" lengths of this, arranged diagonally in rows. This allowed the wrinkles to curve back and forth as they were pushed down on the tape. I found it easiest to start at the bottom row, peeling the papers, arranging and pushing down the wrinkles. Then remove the papers from the second row and repeat, pulling the wrinkles the other direction. When finished, press which holds it permanently in place. Turn the piece over the cut off all excess around the edges.

After sewing shoulder and side seams of the vest and lining, and pressing them open, put the two units together, wrong sides touching. Pin and stay stitch all edges close to the edge. This is bound with a bias piece of the same chiffon cut 2 1/2" wide. Fold in half lengthwise and press a crease. Begin at the underarm side seam on the vest's lower edge, and pin the two raw edges of the binding to the vest raw edges, right sides together. Curve the binding end down and off the project.

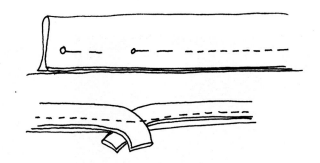

Stitch a 1/4" seam, removing the pins as you approach them. When all the way around, curve the binding other end downwards, generously overlapping. Trim off those ends. Fold the folded edge of the binding around to the vest backside so it covers your original stitching line, and pin from the right side to hold the binding in place underneath. Stitching in the ditch on the right side, and remove the pins as you come up to them. This stitching won't show on the right side, but will on the backside where it holds the binding in place.

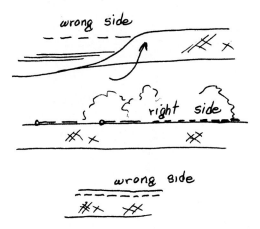

When I tried it on, the vest looked bulky at the back waist, as though it needed some shape, however darts will distort the wrinkles. The perfect solution was in my treasure collection. Six decorative cube beads about 1/2" in size, in purple and metallic gold had been there forever, awaiting this project. A tube of the chiffon, leftover from button loops on the vest front, is strung through all the beads. A knot is tied at each end, as well as between each bead. These knots are hand stitched to the vest at about 2" intervals, producing gathers between each. Anytime I see interesting objects like this in shops I buy them - frequently with nothing definite in mind. Sooner or later they come in handy.

The fact that several fabrics are combined in this pin woven vest allow it to coordinate with many outfits. It will look as though it was created specifically for each. Combining fabrics opens up endless possibilities in your closet - giving you coordinates you never suspected.

Are you ready for something really wonderful? Look at the photo of Grace France's pin woven jacket to really brighten up your day. Seeing and feeling it up close gives an unbelievable amount of pleasure. It's an uplifting event. Not too surprisingly it has won in a couple of prestigious shows. Grace is a retired university professor who can now devote full time to her wearable art where she can display it in her native Montana and in many other places around the country.

This is a vest with sewn-in sleeves. The vest uses a marvellous cotton striped fabric that looks like it is all strip pieced, but isn't. It provides the color combination, is the vest's front lining (back is solid color), and in a big cross section, is pleated down the vest back.

The sleeves are woven as a big piece about 18" x 28", with the long dimension the only edge stitched to the vest, over the shoulder. The strips in this weaving are mainly from the striped fabric, cut on the straight, but pulled through a bias tape maker. Strips of Ultra Suede and some ribbons, as well as novelty yarns are mixed in very happily. All this is fused to a backing, then as an extra and very wise precaution, Grace also stitched curvy lines in monofilament thread throughout so they don't show, but certainly make it sturdy.

See Photo 1405 Page 25

Eyelash yarns are tied all over for a shaggy feathery finish. Dozens of buttons, beads, jewels, shisha mirrors, and little dangley trinkets are hand sewn all over the finished sleeves. The overall effect is breathtaking! When you look it over doesn't it make you want to rush into your sewing room and create such a beauty yourself? Do you feel your sewing becomes rather humdrum? Put together a dazzler like this, and begin a new life!

1406b – Jeanette Bussard's scrap outfit began as an Indian blanket made into a coat.

1406a – The background is a beige linen graced by a collage of silk, wool, cotton and lace appliqués, by Alice Kool.

1406d – "Autumn Cascade" is a collection of brown beige and gray wools to produce this leafy profusion stitched freeform on the machine. By Joy Busch.

1406c – This is a fantastic crazy quilt, put together by a woman of adventurous spirit – Ann Fortin.

1406e – This wonderful coat and jacket are pieced in triangles one by one, by June Greig.

Scrap Happy

I just finished a project of a sleeveless shell of a crepe-backed satin in a nice heavy weight. A square of about 18" and a few other little strips were left over. While I was putting this little bundle away on the dull grey-green-blue shelf, I noticed a piece of the identical color of a jacquard woven floral design. Under that were four scraps about 12" each of a crinkled painted fabric.

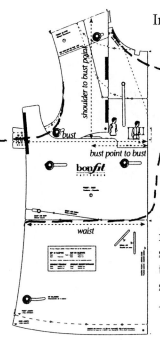

Immediately a vest came to mind. The crinkled pieces would be the center of a log cabin. The two other fabrics would form the surrounding logs, to fill out and cover the pattern piece. Some great buttons in the drawer begged to join this grouping. Two buttons were large and a matching button was smaller. To mix sizes like this suggests that they be somewhat separated. Adding an exaggerated overlap at the top of the vest's right side would accommodate the two larger buttons and seemed like a good plan, while placing the little one at the waist.

I first cut out the fronts and back of the vest in a fusible tricot interfacing. My thought was to fuse the crinkled piece to its center, and then build the surrounding logs by stitching a log right sides together, then flip up and fuse, and then turn over the piece to cut off the excess fabric. The problem was that I had very little fabric, and so couldn't afford to do anything this wasteful. I'll save that log cabin idea for a later project.

The actual project evolved into something quite different. I ended up stretching the wrinkled fabric out, somewhat, wrong side up, and pinning its edges to the ironing board padding. I covered this with a piece of fusible tricot and fused it in place. The size and shape of the crinkled piece is now set and no longer moves.

Chapter 6

The vest pieces were cut from cotton muslin, as a base. As I wanted to check the fit, I first pinned it together for try-on and adjustment. It would be wasteful to cut the fabric off at each seamline, with so little fabric available. My next step was to stitch the muslin shoulders and side seams together, in order to build the project "in the round", instead of the usual "on the flat".

A dress form is really handy, so that all the little fabric pieces can be pinned in place before stitching. If you don't have one, a good substitute is a cutting mat or piece of cardboard. Anything that can be slipped inside to separate the vest back and front will work well. This way you can pin all fabric pieces to the backing fabric without catching the vest back and front together.

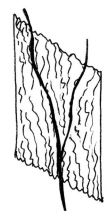

Another idea switch quickly occurred. This would work better if the wrinkled pieces weren't left in their diamond shapes, but could be cut up here and there into curvy pieces, flowing with the wrinkle pattern. These were arranged all over the back and fronts of the vest, in the way that worked out best according to the spacing. Cover the remaining areas with the cut-up crepe-back satin, going in any grain direction necessary to fit the space.

To sew curvy seams with limited fabric is very difficult. The easiest way to do the seams is to simply overlap one fabric edge over its neighbor. Use whatever fabric on top where the topstitching won't be noticeable. The top edge can then be folded under 1/4", pinned in place, removing each pin as you come to it when stitching.

From the third fabric (the jacquard) I made several bias cut fabric tubes. I turned them over a Fasturn brass tube. This fabric cannot be pressed flat. You'll notice that even when pressed the tubes pop back to appear 3-dimensional. Place these tubes, which are stitched on from the underside, so no stitching shows, and to anchor all layers together, over the satin areas to hold that fabric in place against the muslin.

There was just enough satin left to cut bias strips, which are folded over yarn and stitched into a piping using a piping foot. This foot can be purchased at your machine dealer's, and it's great for making a very uniform piping. Place this at the garment edge, raw edges together, and machine baste on the same stitching line.

I chose to line this vest by pinning all around the outer edge, with the lining and vest right sides together. Stitch this, retracing the former stitching line. Grade the edges so each layer is trimmed a slightly different width. As its an inside curve, clip the neckline curve, which would otherwise pull. Turn the vest right-side-out, through an armsyce opening. The outlining piping will now have its finished side showing. Press the edges flat.

The armscyes can be finished either by hand or machine. Turn the piped edge so the finished part is in place, and press it in that position. Clip at the underarm curve, if necessary. Turn the lining edge under (also clipping), and pin, then whip in place with little invisible hand stitches. Another way is to fold under the lining edge, ensuring the fold line slightly covers the piping stitching line. Stitch in the ditch, right side up… on the seam well where the piping and vest meet. This is invisible on the outside of the vest. On the inside, the machine stitching would show close to the lining fold.

There are many other ways to stitch and turn a vest lining - shown previously in other programs.

This vest turned out to be something with a dynamic impact - created almost entirely of scraps! I wouldn't want a whole big coat which would be as dramatically detailed. This is the attraction of a vest. It's a small garment which can be classed as an accessory. You can go wild -playing out elaborate fantasies. Wear it over something plain to tone down the vest. This way it's only an accent - like the spice added to bland food- but it certainly puts a playful zing in your life, without being outlandish.

The outfit worn under the vest is a long sleeved top and pants in velour, but in the identical gray-blue-green color. This was an accidental, but perfect match. I'm all ready for a party - but in need of an invitation!

Color Photo page 52.

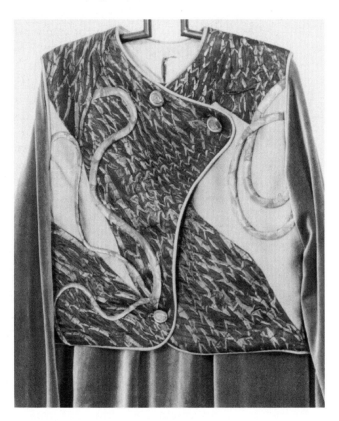

What kind of scraps do I have left over? In putting them all together, like a jigsaw puzzle, I couldn't cover this page. It does the heart good to recycle otherwise useless little bits and pieces into a spectacular accent.

The underlying velour outfit requires special consideration before cutting out and during construction. The first decision to be made is which direction the pile will go. Napped fabrics don't give you a choice. The nap should go down for better wear, to keep a new look. If the nap is cut in the up direction it roughs up, pills more easily and quickly looks old. These fabrics, usually wool or wool blends have been brushed during manufacturing so the little short fiber ends go in the same direction

With pile fabrics such as velvets, velveteens or knit velours, an extra set of yarns have been interwoven separate from the base fabric. These extras are cut, producing the pile surface. When this pile smooths in the downward direction it is a lighter color - a frosty look. If the smooth direction is up, a deeper richer color results. Depending on personal preference, either direction is correct, but the up direction is the most typically chosen. The best way to make your decision is to drape the length of fabric around your neck, standing in front of a mirror. With both directions visible hanging down your front, determine your favorite look. **Ensure you cut out all pattern pieces in the same direction.** The one exception would be if you are making something in patchwork, and the variety would then be desirable.

A very simple styling is suitable when using these knit velours. There is little reason to break up the luxurious expanse of fabric with complicated seaming. The seams will be another consideration. These choices are to finish or not. Being a knit, there is no threat of raveling, and some varieties will lie very flat. If yours is like this you may choose to leave it alone on the edges. Other types curl crosswise to the backside, and lengthwise to the front. This should be prevented, as it will not look good.

Experimenting on a scrap will show you the best look for your particular fabric. Maybe serging each edge, stitching the seam, then pressing open will look the best. Another option is to stitch the seam, then serge the two edges together to prevent curling. You might do this operation all in one by using a 4-thread serger to stitch the seam while serging the edges together. In commercially made garments this would be the usual finish . If you haven't a serger, then try two rows of stitching to accomplish the same thing. Trim close to the outer line.

Another idea is to stitch a seam, trim one short, and press both allowances in that direction so that the short seam is enclosed, and then topstitch. This will keep everything flat, while

eliminating some bulk. To avoid roughing it up, topstitching should be done in the smooth pile direction. Since each fabric could demand something different, samples are the only sure way of deciding on the best technique.

Pressing will also require some sampling to decide on either steam (probably) or dry. Will the smooth surface of the ironing board mash the fabric surface? These pile fabrics frequently iron and look better with some texture under them, such as a terry cloth towel or a needle board. The seams on my fabric simply opened up flat without pressing.

Whether in a pant or skirt outfit, a waistline is probably best handled with a fold over a top casing, housing elastic for a pull-on garment. This doesn't mean the garment will be bulky at the waist in order to be large enough to go over the hips. Remember these knits have crosswise stretch to accommodate the mountain it must slide over before reaching the smaller valley!

For the hem, will it look best to serge the edge, then blind hem machine stitch between layers, or will a hand stitch between layers, about 1/2" down from the edge, be less visible? If seams are topstitched, the best way might be to duplicate this look on a shallow hem, with either one or two rows of stitching.

If a neck opening is needed, an invisible zipper, with nothing but the tab showing, works best. Coats and Clark produce a huge color range of these in all lengths. If this is a dressy outfit you might even consider a crystal zipper. With no stitching showing, this could be applied by slashing 1/2" shorter than the zipper length, then diagonally out to corners. Stitch each side from the seam side on top, through the seam and zipper tape only. We (The Sewing Connection) have these in 6" and 10" lengths - call for availability.

Buttonholes or buttonloops could close the

neckline. If loops, consider making little bias cut tubes in a silky fabric of harmonizing color. Another choice would be twisted thread, done on your bobbin winder. This means using a few strands of any matching color, cut in lengths about 3-4 times longer than needed. If you are using a heavy cord, less will be required. A mixture of thread types is interesting. Insert their ends all together through the center hole of a bobbin, clamping down on the bobbin winder. This won't work if you use too many threads, which rules out big cords. Hold the thread ends out together in one hand. Push the power pedal and let these wind tightly enough that you feel your hand being pulled back closer to the machine. Stop winding. Using your other hand, place a finger on the center of the twisted cords. Ease your right hand in closer, and it will back-wind at that center point. Tie a knot of all the loose ends to keep this ply twisted. If cutting apart, machine stitch back and forth a double row of stitches between each button loop. Determine the button-loop sizes by the size of the button, making sure they will loop over, plus seams. These will be stitched between garment and facing, raw edges aligned with the fabric edge.

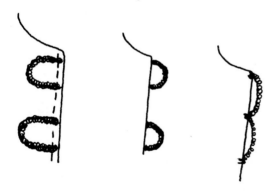

When the fabric is turned right side out, they will pop out into the proper position. Another way to do this is by leaving this twisted as one piece, if you want the buttons close together. Anchor at intervals with small bartacks, to the garment edge.

Back this with an interfaced facing. It might be smart to cut it in a thin silky fabric or lining rather than a second layer of velour, if you want to eliminate bulk. In the neck shaping, I usually cut out fusible interfacing, in an elongated extension at the button opening.   Fuse that to the fabric

(facing) back, and cut it out at the interfacing edge. This is easier than cutting it out separately and getting these small pieces to mesh.

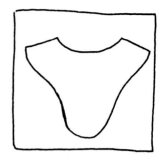

See Photo 1406a Page 28

Some wonderful garments shown on this program were on loan from several talented fiber artists. Alice Kool is from Victoria, B.C. None of these garments were necessarily made of scraps, and perhaps every piece of fabric in the garment was especially purchased for this garment. On the other hand it may remind you of some treasures you already have. Alice won first prize with this Koos van den Aker type piecing in a contest sponsored by BC Woman Magazine and In Stitches. The background is a beige linen graced by a collage of silk, wool, cotton and lace appliques. All their edges are covered by a checked grey bias tape for a beautiful finish.

See Photo 1406b Page 28

On this program another scrap outfit, designed by Jeanette Bussard of Elgin, Minnesota, was shown. It began as an Indian blanket made into a coat for Jeanette's mother. She then took a wearable art class to find some ideas for turning those wonderful wool scraps into something useful. What resulted is a terrific coat, vest and skirt, made by combining the blanket pieces with army green denim, other wools and a variety of trims.

It all coordinates so well you have to admire Jeanette's courage in creating these garments. This is something you can do, too. Color coordinate a little of this and that in your sewing room, and see how quickly something wearable begins to take shape.

See Photo 1406c Page 28

Some of us have scraps, while others have unbelievably wonderful little treasures - a big combination of which will produce something magical. Ann Fortin of Lindale, Texas is in this latter category. It's Ann's mind and fingers that produce the end result of which others wouldn't even dream.

The turquoise rectangular cape exterior is one piece of mohair, with its lining combining several fabrics. Under it the pants are a really nice heavy weight of washed rayon. The top is a blend of that, along with tiny pieces of silks, velvets, cotton, leather, cord, braids, endless hand stitching and beading, producing something awesome. This is a fantastic crazy quilt, put together by a woman of adventurous spirit. In a former life Ann was a princess straight out of the Arabian Nights!

See Photo 1406d Page 28

Joy Busch of Sante Fe is widely known for her wearable art, of which her "Autumn Cascade" is a splendid example. A collection of brown, beige and gray wools join forces to produce all this leafy profusion stitched freeform on the machine. The panels of wool are all beautifully edged with other wool bias strips, all mounted on a muslin base. Antique brass buttons accent here and there, for a marvelous collage. This is certainly an adventurous garment. What an innovative, useful end product for all those leftovers in your stash!

Many scraps of somber wools are combined in this <u>color-blocked</u> June Greig coat but the most unique feature is still to come. After this was all seamed and pressed, every seamline is covered over with <u>hooks, eyes and snaps.</u> The hardware lends a sense of humor only seen at close range.

See Photo 1406e Page 28

For years June worked for an upscale retailer. One day the men's alteration department asked if she'd like to have some cutoff pieces from hemming men's pants. Look at the photo to see what a windfall of these menswear pieces produced! The wonderful coat and jacket pieced in triangles one by one, baby blocks on the other can be mixed and matched with the flying geese on a short skirt, a long skirt, shorts and pants. All coordinate beautifully. Notice her attention to attractive scale. On the coat the triangles are smaller at the shoulders, growing larger down in the flared wide area of the swing coat. All its joinings are outlined by a couched yarn.

Keep in mind there is no law about using several yards of the same fabric in a garment. I hope that some of these examples inspire you to look through your stash and see what might develop when you mix a little of this and that together. Whether mine, or on loan from other talented contributors, there are many garments made wholly or partially from old friends in the closet, which are seen throughout all The Sewing Connection series. As I frequently travel and see what other sewers, quilters, and wearable artists are doing I am reminded to "lighten up". Put more fun in your sewing and let your personality shine.

Organizing Your Space   Chapter 7

At live seminars, I am continually asked one question: How do you organize your personal sewing room? Although the answer is simple it took me a long time before I hit upon the obvious: Suitable storage space makes all the difference!

The surroundings you always see are not my personal space, but a television studio with huge counters on which I work. They wouldn't fit into most sewing rooms. You may be fortunate to have a large sewing room dedicated alone to sewing. You may have a corner of a family room, a bedroom, a dining room. What will work, no matter what your circumstances? Flexible furniture..expandable furniture!! Furniture that has space to store every item in such a way that you can always find it. Furniture that closes up into a compact unit to conceal it's function, if located in a multipurpose room. Furniture that can be updated with your needs. Furniture with all sorts of options; you can attach together to design a large or small space.

You also require a work surface, as well as storage room for your machine and serger. You'll need an ironing, as well as a cutting, area. My favorite piece is a chest with many shallow drawers which I use to organize everything from marking pens to buttons and threads. To alleviate the mess after finishing the project, immediately replace used objects in their drawers. Deep drawers provide poor visibility when small pieces fall to the bottom to immediately become covered by patterns, scissors, and scraps.

Let me show you what I keep in these drawers, and as I open each one, I'll share a sewing tip from that drawer.

Thread Drawers

Depending on how much you sew, you may need a whole thread cabinet. I have several drawers of thread, all colors of the rainbow, arranged for easy location of the exact color I need. One drawer is all cool colors - blue, green, purple, black, white, gray. The next is warm colors - red, orange, pink, yellow, beige, brown. Wooden dowel rows keep all the spools in neat little rows.

These can be purchased in any hardware store or lumber yard. They sit on the bottom to separate rows of spools and are not attached to the drawer. Replace each used spool into its row and you never have to search for thread - in your sewing room - again. Pull the thread end into the spool slot so you don't have tails tangling.

All my general purpose sewing threads are in two drawers, the warm and cool, as mentioned. In a third drawer are the embroidery threads, acrylic and rayon. In another drawer I keep metallic and novelty threads. A slightly deeper fifth drawer houses all the serger threads. Group the four cones of each color together for instant locating.

If you haven't got a magic chest of shallow drawers, life will be easier if you divide things similarly in some other way. Perhaps you can use clear plastic covered tote boxes as a substitute. Some people like to have a peg wall to hold all these things out in the open. Not I!. Think light fading, think lint and dust. I want all mine closed away.

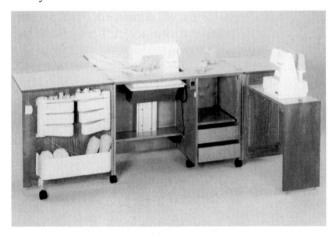

Marking and Measuring Drawer

It is astounding how many rulers, hem or seam gauges, measuring tapes, and other similar devices you have in your sewing supplies! It is most satisfying to have them all collected together in this drawer. For those measuring tools which are too large - yardsticks, L squares, etc. - store them together elsewhere. In this drawer I also keep pocket formers, bias tape markers, point turners, buttonhole spacers (any logical piece of equipment that measures).

There's another huge group for the marking function, including a multitude of fabric marking pens, soapstone, soap slivers, chalk pencils, chalk wheels, chalk powder, refills, marking wheels, carbon sheets and plain old pencils. If it marks, then its in this drawer.

I keep a measurement card containing sizes and the dates on everyone for whom I sew. The grandchildren keep growing so the numbers have to be replaced or adjusted every year. With the adults, well, we hope those measurements don't keep growing. If they do, I want to know before sewing a new project for that person.

Make this chart as complete as necessary. Do you only need bust, waist, and hips? Do you perhaps want to know preferred lengths of skirts and pants? How wide is the shoulder from neck out to shoulder point? What is the neck circumference? How long should sleeves be for blouses, for jackets? Where are the quirky bumps and bulges (like one higher hip) or notes like "darts rounded in front, straight in back"? A simple card per person (or yourself) with this information, as well as their colors or fabrics, and you are always prepared.

Cutting Devices Drawer

Fabric cutting shears, little thread snips, applique scissors, specialty scissors like curved blades for machine embroidery and about fifty other varieties are all found in this drawer. I keep a multitude of rippers there, from a wicked looking surgical curved job to simple plastic ones. From Coats and Clark, I have a lighted ripper that is a pocket penlight with 2 caps; one a ripper and one a needle threader. This works great on dark thread on a dark fabric on a dark night - or tired eyes!

In this drawer are the Fiskars' big and little soft cutters that are so easy on the hands because of their spring action. Also from Fiskars, are the molded handles for comfort and ease to soothe arthritic hands, and ease harshly rubbing off skin when you cut a lot. I might have 50 years worth of scissors here, but I find myself gravitating to these

orange handles as my first preference.

There are also wire-cutting and pinching-plier type tools, as well as needle nose pliers. Craft knives are sometimes the only tool for the job. The wedge type push knife and its wood block under the fabric are the greatest for cutting open machined buttonholes. There are also sharpening tools for any of the above. Hole punchers of various sorts are handy, as is an awl, when you only want to gently push fabrics aside to create a hole, not cut any thread. I see pinking shears looking forlorn because they always chew the fabric while killing your hand. I've found better tools, such as Fiskars pinking and wave blades used interchangeably in their rotary cutters. The first on the market seemed modeled after a pizza cutter. The newest are beautifully designed, with their intelligently engineered handle angled just right, to be user-friendly.

A cutting tip? When buying any cutting tool, try it out to see which feels right. This is really important if a lengthy cutting session is planned. If packaged, see if the shop has a pair unwrapped for you to try.

Hand Sewing Materials Drawer

For anything needed to be sewn by hand, here's the drawer for all those supplies. Snaps of all sizes in silver, black and clear plastic are here. Small wire hooks and eyes, as well as hefty skirt or pants hooks are in their own little clear plastic boxes. There will also be straight pins, safety pins, and every size and type of hand sewing needles. In its plastic slotted holder, you'll have beeswax to prevent your thread from knotting as well as strengthening it. Curved safety pins are great for basting layers together before quilting.

When the needle won't easily go through a resistant fabric, use a little rubber circle to fold over it, preventing slippage and ease of pulling through. If the fabric is still stubborn, use a little plier clamp to do the job.

One of my favorite needles is a tapestry needle. Although I have packages of them in the drawer, I always have one next to my machine. This needle has many uses, including helping develop roundness, easing in a thread where needed in bust front edge or armscye. The blunt point goes beautifully at intervals under the stitching thread to pull it up and work in fabric fullness. Another way to utilize the tapestry needle is to thread a serger chain through its big eye, once the blunt point has been inserted between the serger stitches and fabric. Pull the chain safely through this, and cut off the extra chain. That safety length is now securely hidden and won't ravel out. This is a good way to end a line if your sensitive skin cannot tolerate the sometimes scratchy bead left by seam sealants.

Machine Sewing Supplies Drawer

I keep all small supplies for the machine and serger which are better stored in a shallow drawer, rather than a large space. The biggest space consumer in this drawer is the large needle collection. I have seen all sorts of innovative ideas for storing up to half a dozen needles that I never understand. I need much more space than that. I want to have at least one package of every size and type of needle available in this drawer. I want many of the most commonly used needles on hand. When I need to replace a needle, I want it in that drawer, not down in a shop. Therefore, I stock up.

There are sometimes instructions in publications about filing a burr off a needle or sharpening it. Is that writer for real? Think of the price of that needle as opposed to the price of the fabric it is ruining by pulling yarns. Think of your time ripping and redoing when the stitches don't look right. Throw out that defective needle and replace it with a new one. A new one for each garment? Not necessarily - if its still good, keep using it. I leave the box next to my machine so I can remember what needle I am using from day to day. If I change needle type or size, I put the old one back into the first slot to tell me next time I get out that package it's a used needle. It really doesn't matter if this needle is new or used. If I put it back in the package it still works like new.

Bobbins are very inexpensive. I like a big supply of them, as it seems silly to unwind thread to get an empty one, to simply rewind with another color.

In this drawer I also keep screwdrivers, cleaning brushes, tweezers - anything small needed for a machine or serger.

Beloved Buttons Drawer

This is probably my favorite drawer, and I can spend endless hours going through it - but I don't need to, for in a flash the perfect button is at my fingertips. Years ago (many years!), my whole button supply was kept in a cookie tin. Then it graduated to something bigger and bigger. I now have the ultimate for happy usage. I discovered these drawers are the exact size of 12 boxes in which my bank checks arrive. Incredible? The right length, width and height - 12 boxes. I label the boxes with the color contained within. As soon as I bring new buttons home they go immediately into the designated color box, and they are always easy to find.

Sometimes you are faced with a chicken-egg situation. Which comes first? Either way.. At times, when I have my fabric in hand, I find the best buttons in the shop for that particular outfit. At other times I just see fantastic buttons of a different color. We pass this way but once. If you love them, buy them, as you may never see them again. I put them away, and no doubt at some future date they'll undoubtedly be a knockout. When I need a button of a particular color I'll check out these boxes before I shop. I usually have several great choices which even suggest what styling changes I'll make on a basic pattern.

Remember - a button shank should be as long as the buttonhole thickness to rest easily, without pulling. This means a thin fabric (blouse) can handle a flat button with holes, no shank. A wool coat would demand a big thread shank on a flat button. Be sure the button shank is sewn on in the same direction as the buttonhole. Big buttonholes of heavy duty garments need horizontal buttonholes, as a vertical would pull out of line. However, a small buttonhole can be vertical as the pull would be negligible. If the garment has a band, the buttonhole must be vertical.

I will happily pay whatever a super button costs because it can really make the outfit just right.

Elastic Drawer

Each time I buy elastic, usually in a big roll, I treat it as if I have never used it before. You frequently hear or read a blanket rule of elasticized

1408 – Recycled Turtleneck.

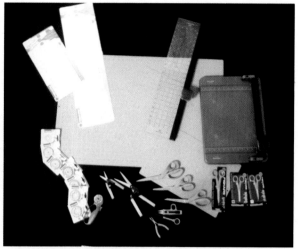

1408 – Some of Fiskars wonderful products.

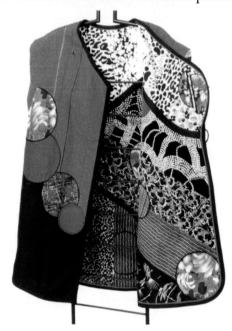

1409b – Bobbie Culbert designed a really interesting reversible vest with an Oriental theme.

1409a – Lethbridge Coulees and hexagon jewerly both inspire this padded design.

1409c – Marian Eller created these two jackets.

waistbands such as "cut it 2 inches smaller than your waistline measurement", or something similar. With some brands you may be in for misery doing this, as they all feel different.

To play it safe try this: pin a length of elastic around your waist over your skin, not over your clothes. Overlap the end an inch or two before cutting it off. Go about your business for several hours. If you forget that elastic belt under your clothes, then you've found the right size. However, it may be excruciatingly painful an hour later. This tells you to loosen up. When correct, trim the elastic down so the ends just touch, not overlap as that overlap is bulky. Pin a piece of twill tape, ribbon, or anything flat under the joining. Zigzag about 3 rows to ensure it never comes apart - one over the joining and one on either side. This will go inside the fabric, turning it down over to stitch in place. Stretch out the waist when all is stitched to distribute the gathers. You might then stitch through at each vertical seam, stitching in the ditch so it doesn't show. This prohibits rolling or shifting.

Now that I know what's comfortable on this first cut from my roll of elastic. I'll cut several more the same size to have them ready for my next project. If you prefer not to cut ahead, measure that length exactly and mark it down on a note attached to the roll.

Seam Sealants, Glues, Sticky Tape Drawer

This is my least used drawer, but it may not be that way for someone else. I just don't glue very much, but sometimes glue is the perfect solution to a permanent or temporary problem.

There are literally dozens, maybe hundreds, of glues on the market. Read the label to decide it is the answer to your needs. If liquid, ensure the container doesn't leak. Make sure glue sticks haven't dried out. Keep all lids and caps tightly in place. Some brands tend to dry out or evaporate with time, so don't be surprised if you discover a four year old never used empty glue bottle.

To apply a minimal amount of liquid, consider dipping a pinpoint into it to transfer that small amount to your fabric. Be sure to let all glues dry on the fabric before adding stitching to the area. Read labels also to see if the glue is washable or dry-cleanable.

General

After using a chest of drawers in this way, you might evaluate your frequency of usage. My two chests are stacked and bolted - 12 drawers high. I can see into the top two drawers when I am standing, not when seated at my machine. Therefore my two top drawers have supplies which are least often used in them.

There are still more drawers, but you get the idea. A workable arrangement of all this storage really lightens your load and makes sewing doubly enjoyable.

I have walls of shelving for storing fabric - all color sorted and neatly folded and stacked behind folding closet doors. Open shelving, covering a couple of walls, hold all my books and videos. I use a tall cabinet next to my ironing board for interfacings, sorted by fusible and non-fusible. All the pressing aids and distilled water jugs are kept there. On the wall, my rotary cutting mats and large measuring boards are stored upright by heavy angled hooks. A flat space holds my Bonfit patterners.

Another large cabinet houses all covered plastic boxes for machine parts, computer memory cards, cords, braids, beads, ribbons, and all manner of other sewing necessities.

Does this sound like rather a large room? Well it is, but remember, sewing is my business as well as my hobby. Whether your sewing space is large or small, organization of storage and work space is the key to making the best possible use of it all. The starting point for you may be to find the furniture which opens up to work, and then folds up into a condensed space for the rest of the time. To help you find the best and most suitable means write:

Horn Collection

Horn of America, Incorporated,
PO Box 608, Sutton, WV 26601
or call: 1-800-882-8845
Tell them Shirley sent you!

Sweaters and Suede   Chapter 8

Victoria is a beautiful city in British Columbia. We flew to Seattle late winter and almost froze our toes waiting in line for the Catamaran ride across the water to Canada. What a wonderful surprise greeted us there. Although further north, it was springtime with everything flowering. There was still a nip in the air and I saw the perfect jacket in a pricey little shop. It was a combination of suede and sweater knit.

Well, you know me. I just shop for ideas, and thought what a neat recycle job this could be, combining an old sweater with synthetic suede. I just happened to have a sweater that exactly matched some rich red suede, so I was in business! The sweater is a heavy ribbed turtleneck, good as a jacket weight.

Don't jump into this too hastily. Consider the possibilities and make choices you'll be happy with. For instance, the sweater needed enlarging. Strips or panels of suede would do this beautifully. Here are some of the thought processes.

How much fabric? When I stood in front of a mirror wearing the sweater I could see more fabric was needed, but I couldn't even guess how much. I needed to open the knit to see how easily it pulled apart, and then would have to measure that open space.

What about pockets? As this was to be a casual jacket, pockets would be good. What kind and where? Patch pockets would pull and sag on the sweater knit while I wanted to avoid slash pockets. The exception would be to locate pockets where the suede and knit joined, thus stabilizing the knit in this manner.

How will this open and fasten? Probably down the center front. Since the sweater is a turtle neck, there will be a generous collar (a real bonus). A band of suede on each front edge will overlap and button.While looking through my red button collection I found all sorts of perfect color matches which complemented the sweater knit and the suede. The problem was that there wasn't enough of any one button. I needed half a dozen. So I chose a less artistic button which had the six I

needed. Compromise is a part of success. Now some ideas started taking shape.

How will this become larger? Had the sweater seams been serged together I might have left them alone and cut open elsewhere along a vertical rib. I might even have trimmed them off to open the sides. However, these were finished pieces, merely sewn together in a very shallow machine stitched seam. The most sensible method to open the knit was to carefully cut each stitch.

Once the sides and sleeves are open, it's an easy matter to again try on the sweater to see how big the gap is on each side when it hangs with sufficient jacket ease. At that point the whole picture came together and I could make logical decisions.

See Photo 1408 Page 37

It would look like this. The open side and sleeve seams would be joined by 4" strips of suede. Pockets welts would go in the seam where the sweater and suede joined with the pocket pieces hanging inside.

A cut up the very center front of the sweater, out through the turtle neck opens the unit for a cardigan. Suede trim enfolds the cut collar edges. 1" wide suede bands at each front edge hold the buttons and buttonholes. Should a suede band be used around bottom and wrist edges? Yes, if it will be lined in order to secure the lining bottom edges. Not necessarily, if it will remain unlined. I personally don't care to see pockets hanging loose inside an unlined jacket, so I will line.

These decisions must be made before beginning your project. They are quickly followed by WHEN must these processes be done. For example, if this jacket is lined, the time to cut out the lining is immediately, while the sides are open. Cut an accurate shape by tracing the flat piece.

Make a quick pattern in just a few minutes on pattern paper or fibrous pattern tracer. An easy way to make an absolutely perfect fit is to lay the pieces out flat on the paper, and trace the body outline. Stick pins on the seamlines of neckline

1409d – June Greig beautifully stitched on this olive wool jersey

1410a – My favorite coats with removable collars.

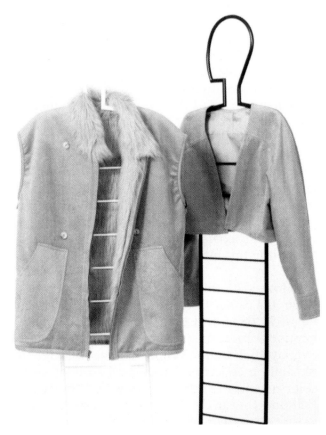

1410b & c – The jacket is a vest plus button-on shoulder sleeves. Would be perfect for skiers.

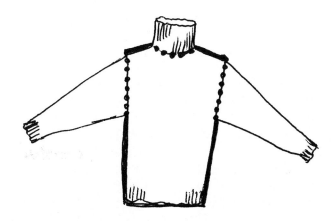

and armscyes through the sweater and paper. Carefully lift up the sweater slightly to mark on the paper where each pin is entering. Remove the sweater and follow the dots to complete the outline. More than likely, the front and back of the sweater are identical, except for the front lower neckline. Trace them both on the same pattern. For efficiency during cutting out, cut two layers of the higher-necked back. Remove one, and re-cut the lower neckline for the front. Cut this front in half down the center, but leave the back in one piece.

Remember to add seam allowances everywhere when cutting out, as well as any additional width you will add at the sides.

With the underarm seam already open, lay the sleeves flat and trace around the outline. Stab pins as before to get the armscye outline. At this time I put my hand on a paper in the position I would have it in that in-seam pocket, and created a pattern that would comfortably accommodate it.

Continuing with the sweater; the starter might be opening up the center front. Stabilize before cutting open, so as not to risk any stretch. Cut two 3" wide strips of fusible interfacing, 1" longer than the sweater center front, from lower edge all the

way up to the turtle neck collar edge. Fuse these strips to the backside of a manmade suede or leather. Cut out and press 1/4" under one edge of each. This will later wrap around to the sweater back edge.

Align these strips at sweater center front, touching edges, with right sides together. For this suede, I used it in the UP direction, providing a deeper, richer color. Stitch a shallow 1/4" seam from the center on each strip. This will stabilize the garment, and make it safe to cut up the center. Press strips out flat, then fold to backside so that the folded edge extends just slightly past the original stitching line. You might stitch the top edge in a small seam before this step so it will be finished. Now stitch-in-the-ditch to connect on the backside, but stitch with the right side up. Press and edge stitch at the fold. This backside would wait to be finished later If lining is used, as it needs to enclose the lining raw edge.

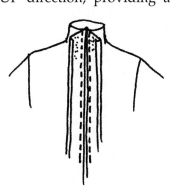

Will embellishments be added? The time for decoration is when the sleeves are opened. Start strips of suede up at the neck, extending down to the wrist. Cut these with a Fiskars rotary wave or pinking blade for a fabulous accent. Look into the new one attached to a long wide ruler. The blade types are just as easily changed in this as they are in the hand held model. An added feature is a rubber

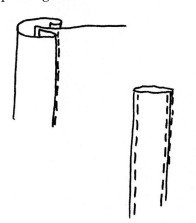

strip underneath the ruler to ensure that nothing slips on the fabric as you cut. Braid narrow straight strips flat, and secure their edges by a straight line of stitching (another thought). Border the center front with the same accents. Consider every idea.

This is the decorative suede addition on mine. Bordering the front band is a 3/8" wide strip of suede cut with the wave blade on the crosswise direction of suede to make it a bit more supple. Next to it is a 3/4" strip, same Fiskars rotary blade. Down its center holes are punched with a snap or gripper tool. Outside that is a row of five shapes cut using a perforated plastic stencil, usually found in quilt shops. The wavy strips were simply stitched on the sweater. To make the S shapes, I fused fabric to a fusible sheet, then cut out the shapes with a straight blade. Peel off the paper backs, arrange them on a 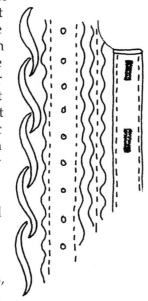 sweater, cover with a press cloth, and fuse in place. Stitch down each close to the edge.

On the shoulders, down to the wrist, the suede decor is similar, cut with a wave blade, alternating with straight and narrow strips. A third straight strip was laced through the perforations after the strip was sewn on.

To enlarge the sweater for a jacket, I cut 4" wide strips the length of sweater side seams, and the same for the length of the sleeve seam.

The sleeve was completely sewn together. The sweater body was mainly finished, leaving only a pocket opening. Insert welt and pocket pieces as follows:

Vertical Welt Pockets

Cut two 7" x 3" strips of suede and fusible interfacing to back each pocket. Fuse and fold each in half lengthwise and stitch each end in a shallow seam. Turn right side out and press. Topstitch the three finished edges, if you like. Cut from this pattern piece you made by drawing around earlier, 4 layers of a lining fabric. With the raw edges together, place a finished welt piece on a lining about 1" down from the top, and stitch in place.

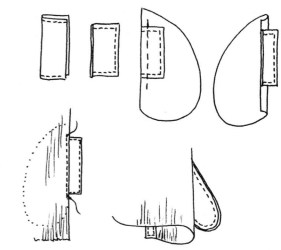

Stitch the two together about 3/8" from the edge. Press the lining back at the stitching line. Position this unit under the side sweater edge so about 1" of welt protrudes. Topstitch to the finished sweater edge, using two lines if desired for stability.

Position the remaining lining pocket piece at the same level under the suede side addition and double topstitch the edge. With the sweater front

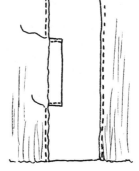 folded out of the way, stitch two rounded lining edges together.

Overlap the sweater, lower end over suede edge, and stitch to join. Topstitch welt top and bottom edges to suede strip on which it rests.

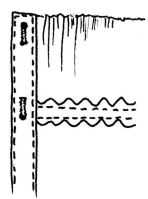

Cut out lining, construct, insert in jacket, staystitching all edges to all sweater edges. The neckline was treated in this way to stabilize and strengthen the sweater so no stretch or strain would occur. The raw lining edge was pinned to the sweater neck. It is covered by a wavy 5/8" strip of suede stitched top and bottom, securing the lining.

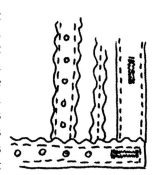

For the lower jacket edge and wrists, I used an interfaced band cut about 2" wide, and pressed in half. It sandwiches the jacket edges for a finished look, using several rows of topstitching. Buttons and machine buttonholes complete the jacket. It makes a coordinated outfit with its skirt of matching suede.

Recycling really is fun, you can be creative while reusing something in a very pretty way!

Two suits made by Betty Haskins of Lexington, Virginia, also used manmade suede with cut suede shapes. The cutouts all the way down the front of the lavender suede were positioned with the nap going the opposite direction, giving a different color impression. On another, the gray suede trim nicely accents the pink and gray mohair suit fabric.

This sweater has an interesting suede use. It was cut of sweater yardage in a novelty knit and assembled. The suede is then on the collar and cuffs. June Greig rolled that rotary cutter many times to cut all these 1/8" strips to knit, using it as yarn.

Only 1 1/2 yds. of this heavy wool was available so none was wasted on seams. They merely butt together with zigzagging, covered by suede. A different color suede on each side makes them reversible as made by June Greig of St. Louis. On one side of the garment cut a narrow strip of suede to stitch in place covering the joining. On the other side, and do this one last, make it wider so the two-sided stitching lines won't show on each other.

These projects were especially easy using the huge variety of Fiskars cutting equipment available. Think about using some of those rotary blades with fancy shapes for belts and bags. Multi strips of one particular shape used over and over on many shades of one color will be quite striking in a bag in chapter 1412.

Lethbridge Leanings *Chapter 9*

Lethbridge is a lovely little city in Alberta, Canada. Not only do I lean toward its charm, but its natives joke that everyone leans because the wind blows constantly! Most programs in this series are inspired by something I saw or experienced in my travels. Lethbridge inspired raised hexagons.

Did these concern the impressive High Level Bridge, spanning a huge chasm? Not really. Have the three dimensions something to do with the coulees lushly swelling over the landscape? These coulees are dreamlike, surrealistic hills which all flow together. Breathtaking, and maybe they did influence the various sized swells somewhat on my jacket.

What actually motivated the shapes is a bracelet and earrings in hexagon shapes, which I bought there. Beyond that was recycling a never worn outfit, languishing in a closet because its fabric looked so limp. To add padding and stitching will beef it up, give it character. Suddenly this throwaway assumes new importance.

Decide by trying it on in front of a mirror, and decide where you want the decorative shapes to be located. To make the hexagon pattern, begin with a square of paper the size of the largest one you want. Fold it in half. From its center, fold about 1/3 of it down to the right. Repeat on the

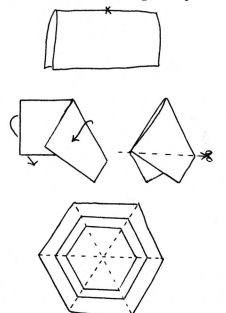

left side so you end up with (roughly) a triangle. Cut off the lower uneven layer edges. Open it up and you will have a perfect hexagon. Draw several other lines in this, each about 1/4 size smaller. This will give you patterns of the same shape in several sizes, as variety is probably more interesting than repeating identical sizes every time. Trace each of these sizes on other papers to make several templates.

From a complimentary fabric, cut several of these shapes in each size. These will be appliquéd to the garment in some arrangement that appeals to you. Any other geometric shape would work just as well - circles, squares, triangles, etc. Any of these shapes are simply easy to repeat, making them larger or smaller.

This is best done on a very simple garment if you plan to recycle, so that it can be worked on without taking it apart. If you are starting from scratch, the choice is yours, anything that works in the flat fabric pieces. My original garment is from a Bonfit patterner basic bodice. It is cut

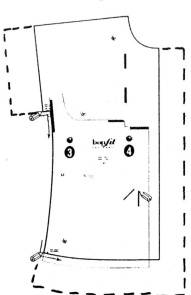

longer for an overblouse. The cut-on sleeve panel is attached and 4" more added to the sleeve when cutting out. 3" was added to the center front producing the big overlap.

A good way to begin is by spreading the right front out on the ironing board, wrong side up. Spread a little fiberfill wherever you have decided the shapes will go. Over this sheet I spread a sheer fusible interfacing, fusible side down. This extended beyond the fiberfill area so that it would be also affixed to the surrounding area of garment fabric. Trim off outer areas of interfacing where none is needed.

With the fabric now prepared, on the garment outside, I arranged the cut-out shapes. These could be fused on and their edges satin stitched in place. I wanted neither this extra stiffness nor the extra thread. The alternative I chose was to fold under each shape edge and finger press them before crisply flattening with a steam iron. Pin

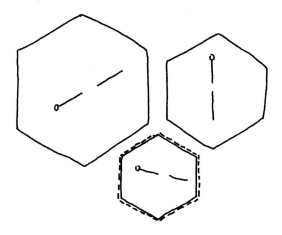

these in place on the garment. A machine appliqué stitch works well. Stitch right next to the folded edge, then takes a narrow swing to the left about every third stitch. It gives the effect of a hand applique but takes a fraction of the time.

Some prefer to stitch to a thin backing fabric, right sides together. Trim off excess, including corners, then cut a big slit on the backing side and turn right side out. Push out all corners and press. I chose the first method as the quickest.

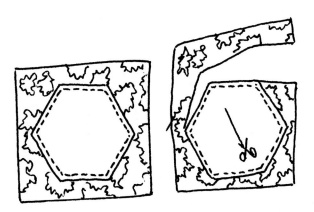

See Photo 1409a Page 37

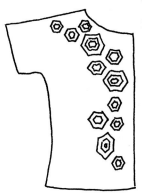

When the applique is finished on the garment the real fun begins - stitched hexagons in metallic thread. The reason I chose a metallic thread was that the print fabric of the skirt and appliqués is overprinted with metallic gold ink. This seems appropriate to tie everything together.

Things evolve. My original intent was to merely stitch two rows around each and position as sketched. They would be in groups interlocking each other. The fiberfill proved too puffy in the blank spaces. More

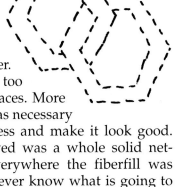

and more stitching was necessary to reduce this puffiness and make it look good. What therefore evolved was a whole solid network of stitching everywhere the fiberfill was fused in place. You never know what is going to happen until the sewing starts. What works in your head often turns out to be a big surprise when done with fabric and machine.

This process became further efficient. It would be tedious to stitch countless hexagons with a beginning and ending of every line. Further evolution developed into a continuous line around each from start to finish. Remember to keep it fun! Never get bogged down in such tedium that you regret ever having started this project.

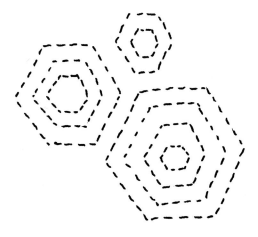

A great aid in constantly turning these corners is the use of a knee lift rather than manually lifting the presser foot, if your machine has this capability. Use the needle in the down position to hold your fabric in place when the foot is lifted.

As it turned out with this garment, the lining seemed superfluous. I usually line a jacket so it will look wonderful inside if I take it off. This is more like a two-piece dress than a suit. Because of this I decided to leave it unlined.

If you like the look of quilted clothing, let's think of other ways that could also be interesting. That three-dimensional look really can add immeasurable interest to a fabric and spice to your wardrobe. The "Dress for Success" look of the 70's was a bore as it allowed no room for creativity. The current theme emphasizes self expression. This is a boon for home sewers because it opens the door for all manner of fulfilling endeavors, creating fun on your sewing machine.

Another possibility along these lines is to find quilting templates in your fabric, quilting or craft shop. These are clear plastic plates with a perforated or slotted design cut in them. Many choices are available. Place these on the fabric layers (cotton, flannel, thin fleece or batting, fiberfill, etc. as a loft beneath the fashion fabric layer). A pouncer is one choice to mark this on the fabric. This is a little fabric packet with chalk dust inside.

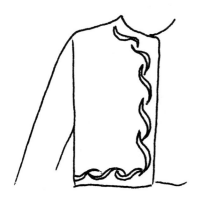

When daubed over the slotted template enough chalk is emitted through the slots to mark the fabric. A marking pen or pencil can be used to trace these designs also. Use this design on a border around the edges of the vest, dress or jacket. Use it repeatedly for a continuous design as these are meant to connect together in this way. After marking, plot your stitching strategy. The goal is to stitch as long a line as possible without starts and stops. Rarely can you get away with backstitching or stitching in place without it showing. The nicest finish is to pull threads to the fabric underside and tie knots. This can be tedious, therefore, try to interrupt these lines as little as possible.

Would you like to see a still easier way to quilt a design? Can you imagine choosing that design, touching that choice on your sewing machine computer display screen and watching the machine stitch it out automatically? We'll do that very process on another program, so keep watching!

See Photo 1409b Page 37

Bobbie Culbert of Santa Fe designed a really interesting reversible vest with a similar appliquéd theme. Circles are the shapes chosen. Bobbi has a business making flamenco dancer costumes. The circular ruffles used profusely in

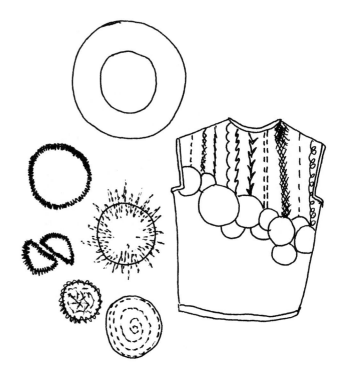

her costumes all leave something behind - the "doughnut holes", in various sizes! Their diameters may vary between 3" across up to about 10".

One side of her vest is all Oriental prints in black and white cottons pieced together in a variety of shapes and sizes. The circles appliquéd here in an assortment of red prints are randomly fused and appliqued with satin stitching or free-motion back and forth stitches to cover edges. Some are split, others have additional interior stitching.

The other vest side is a solid black on the lower part. The upper section is solid red, but all are vertically stitched with automatic machine capabilities. The joining line is covered with a profusion of the circles. Bobbie probably planned it this way, but it might be an idea to use when you run short of fabric.

I love it when sewers and quilters collide. We all learn so much from each other and can adapt ideas from either discipline to incorporate into our own work.The quilters especially seem to have a "lighten up" attitude that helps the serious sewer to have more fun. With quilted clothing becoming so popular we all do a lot more fabric mixing, as evidenced in ready to wear.

The "art-to-wear" sewers mix all sorts of techniques from every type of needlework and open up a whole new area - the garment inside. This is usually as enjoyable as the garment outside. This exposure encourages you to be more adventurous. Lining doesn't have to be solid colored fabric from the lining department. It may be the perfect place to combine several leftover fabrics from past projects for a lively interior.

See Photo 1409c Page 37

Marian Eller of Houston created the two jackets photographed together. The red and gold printed silk is a little reminiscent of the Lethbridge coulees in its circular design. Many of these she has lightly padded with fiberfill and hand-stitched around them to hold in place. Others are outlined with beads to make a really lovely jacket.

Marian's second jacket is an Oriental cotton print in orange, beige, black and gold. On all these colors is a shadowy charcoal overprint of characters. These she outlined with a straight stitch connecting the fabric to its cotton flannel backing and later stuffed them through a slash in the backing fabric. In between, the whole jacket is covered with stipple stitch that creates a beautiful, dramatic mood in copper thread. Again, here is that padded quilted look that adds so much dimension.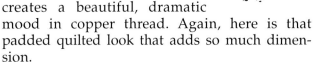

See Photo 1409d Page 40

June Greig of St. Louis has a different type trapunto beautifully stitched on this olive wool jersey. This is also sewing two layers of fabric together in the chosen design - here intertwined figure 8's. After stitching, little slits are cut where necessary and with the big-eyed, blunt-tipped tapestry needle fat yarn is pulled through. As you go around curves simply come back out where necessary to change needle direction.

Create some coulees of your own either for their visual effect, or to make a fabric behave as you would prefer. This three dimensional effect can make every fabric even more interesting.

Posh Pastel Furs   Chapter 10

Remember back in series 13 I had this magnificent idea of fur collars dyed to match some leather coats and jackets. These would be terrific on a wool melton or a tweed. I've seen them in shops and catalogs so obviously it can be done.

I tried it.

I dyed it.

White faux fox fur in the washer with strong dye. Afterwards out of the washer came —you guessed it — white fur! It would take no color!

See Photo 1410a Page 40

Well guess what? It is now possible to purchase fur in several colors and I just couldn't resist. Look at the photo for what has happened. My favorite pewter leather coat turns to cold weather with a blue fox shawl collar. My frequently worn but will-never-wear-out metallic orchid jacket sports a lavender shawl collar. The collarless burgundy leather is now cozy with a pink fur round collar.

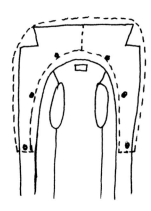

For patterns to make button-on collars, simply duplicate the existing collar on your coat or jacket, if there is one. For example, the two coats with fur shawl collars actually have notched collars hiding beneath. Flatten out your collar and lapels on a tape over pattern tracer or paper and trace the outer edge. Ignore the notch and simply smooth out that outside style line. At about the waistline the shawl collar will terminate. Line this and put button-loops where pictured in the above figure. The clear plastic buttons sewn inside of the coat will never really even be noticed when the fur collar is not being used.

For the collarless coat you can do something similar, tracing the neckline. Remove the coat and arbitrarily draw the outer style line as wide or narrow as you choose. This will produce a flat collar.

Chapter 10

If you would prefer a snugly collar that stands up somewhat on your neck before it folds down, tighten up the outer style line. To do this just fold in at about the shoulder seams what looks like darts on each side of perhaps 1" folds on the outer edge, tapering to nothing on the neck edge. The photo actually has a flat collar. This change would have made it much better.

See Photo 1410b & 1410c Page 40

The pale green convertible vest-jacket photographed would be perfect for skiers as well as many others. I know I'll get a lot of letters asking what pattern it is. It's not a commercial pattern but one you make yourself.

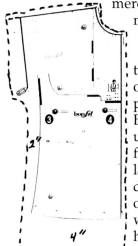

Begin with a large tee shirt type pattern left sleeveless, opened in front for a zipper. Let's explain this on the Bonfit patterner which I used as my basic. With the fur's bulk it will have to be large enough to accommodate the fur inside and the outer suede shell. I also want it longer and looser to have room for a heavy sweater beneath it. By wrapping the uncut fur around me and measuring the resulting girth, I decided to make this 8" larger and 4" longer than the patterner when this is set for my size. This meant sliding the side seams out, each 2" for the 8" total as illustrated in this diagram.

1411b – June Greig woven vest.

1411a –Woven jacket from Wendy Hahn.

1411 – Another jacket from hand woven fabric.

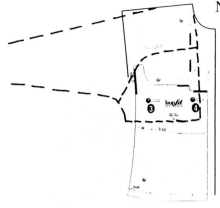

Notice the cut-on sleeve panel is used for drop shoulders.

The button-on abbreviated jacket is also made from the same base. It is shortened to waist length and comes straight down from side neck at the center front. The sleeves are extended down to the wrist and tapered. This unit will only have lining fabric inside, not additional fur but must be large enough to fit over the vest unit. On suedes and leather lots of top stitched seams are attractive. A raglan line cut front and back is simple enough. Remember to add seam allowances wherever new seams are cut.

Now that we have the patterns settled, let's cut out and construct. If you have any qualms about the pattern, its always a good idea to make it up in an ugly old fabric first to be sure it will work as you had planned. The more you do your own patterns, the more sure you become of the successful outcome of your project.

To cut the fur, you will only cut the knit backing, not cutting through the hairs along with it. Be sure to lay all your pattern pieces with the fur going in the down direction on the knit backing. You could also trace lines directly from the patterner onto the fabric and bypass the middleman paper pattern.

First consider those removable collars. As you look at them think how the smooth fur direction should go. If it would seem wise to cut them all in one piece, reconsider. To have the fronts going down, the back would then go up. It is better for all of these pictured to have a center back seam. This enables you to lay the pattern so the center back goes sideways, fronts downward.

Cut the fur against the grain and you will have no mess when you finish as the hairs can safely be avoided. With the knit backing on top keep your shears titled slightly upward so that the point of the underneath blade parts the hair

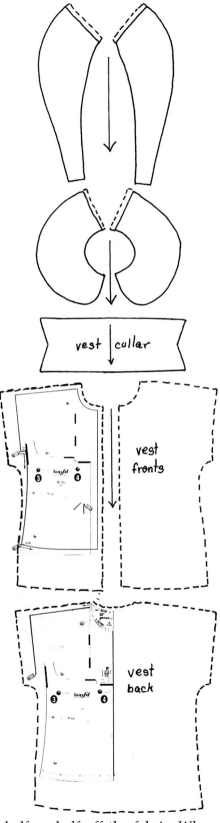

and you cut knit only. 1/4" seams are needed in the fur as any wider is only bulky.

Once all fur pieces are cut out stitch the collar center back seam or the vest shoulder and side seams. To stitch these put right sides together, smooth all the edge fur down between the layers, pin the start. Zigzag over the edge starting from the top and stitching in the down direction. If your machine has the capability, use the needle down position so every few stitches you can stop and the needle will hold the fabric in place while you adjust the fur between layers. This should be a medium width zigzag half on half off the fabric. When finished it will open up flat, rather like a hinge. You cannot press the fur as it will melt. Just smooth each seam out flat with your hand.

If you plan on making the removable collars, the lining will merely be a duplicate of the fur pieces. Stitch them together after interfacing the lining. Again, tuck fur between the layers while stitching leaving an opening somewhere. Turn right side out, close the opening by hand and probably the outer edges can be sufficiently flattened from the lining side with a clapper. Some of mine are lined with FabuLeather and if need be, a little hand understitching can be done to flatten those edges. Buttonloops, hand crocheted or machine twisted are added to coincide with buttons inside the jacket.

To cut out the suede vest and overjacket, decide in advance whether you prefer to have the suede nap going in the up or down direction. Cut all pieces consistently the same way. These can be stitched just as any other fabric and pressed with a steam iron and press cloth. The same is true if you use FabuLeather except there is no nap to be concerned about. On either, topstitching at every seam is an attractive finish to both and to give it a leather look as well as making it very flat. Add patch pockets to this suede side if you like.

Once the suede and fur units are each completed, what remains is a fur collar, a zipper, and perhaps bindings at the armscyes and lower edge. The order in which you do this is up to you as there are several options.

This order worked well for me. At the center front fur edges trim off 1" of fur. To avoid get-

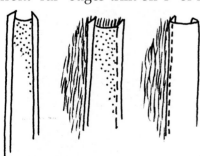

ting it caught in the zipper operation a suede band attaching fur to zipper is a good idea. Cut the bands 1 & 1/2" wide and interface each. Press under 3/8" on each long edge as no pressing can be done after the fur is attached. Topstitch one edge of these directly to each front fur edge, or do this in two steps first seaming in the pressed crease, then topstitching to hold it flat.

Next choose a zipper. Separating zippers come in a large color and length range and you should come fairly close to your suede color.   If

looking for a reversible zipper in case you want to wear the vest with the fur side out, the selection might be limited to neutral colors. I chose a one-sided zipper in a harmonious color. To the back side of this the suede band is topstitched, exposing the zipper teeth and a little of the tape.

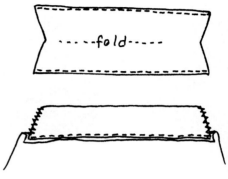

Then the fur collar is sewn on, one long edge stitched to the fur neck-line, the other to the suede. Then, fur sides together, zigzag over the edges of each end. Turn the collar right side out and the fur unit fits nicely inside the suede unit.

Staystitch the two units together, wrong sides touching at the lower edge and around the armholes. Pin the suede unit whose center front edge has a 5/8" seam allowance pressed under over the zipper tapes. The folded edge of the suede should coincide with the edge of the zipper teeth. This

will produce a concealed zipper on the suede side even though it is an exposed zipper on the fur side. I did this to distribute bulk and make its operation efficient.

From cross-cut strips of suede (for a little stretch capability, bind the armscyes. These are 1" wide but as you wrap around the edge, make the backside just a tiny bit larger to be sure both front and back strip edges will be caught when stitched in one operation. I stretched this strip slightly when pinning and stitching it on to draw in those sleeve and lower edges somewhat. These edges could have been finished without the bands, just sewing them together. The fur would show below on the suede side, however, so the bands are there to extend the suede and cover up.

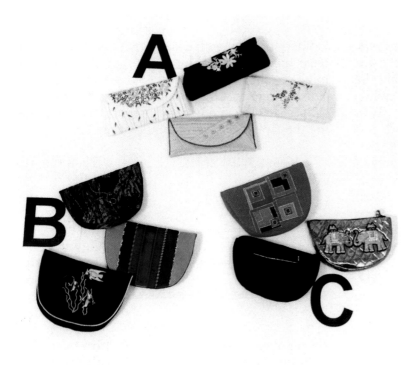

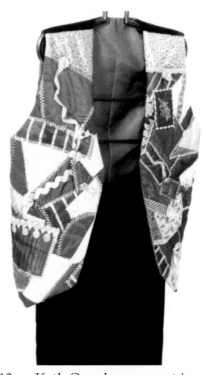

1412 – The Sewing Connection – "The Clutch".

1413a – Kath Ongelmeyer vest in metallics, lace, silks, and velvets.

Velour outfit.

1413b – Quilted vest surrounded by some harmonizing pieces to produce a wardrobe symphony.

The button-on jacket is quickly constructed treating the suede or leather as any other fabric. Again, double rows of topstitching at every seam look terrific and hold it all very flat. The inside is lining fabric sewn out to the edge. There are 7 buttonholes as illustrated, 2 on each center front, one at the back neck, and one under each arm. Sew buttons on the vest in corresponding locations to transform the vest to a jacket.

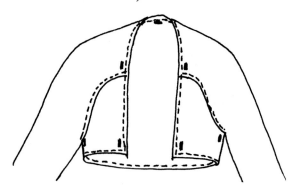

A little tassel attached to the zipper pull completes it. The tassel is more of the suede in a strip about 3" x 3", most of the length cut into a deep fringe. Roll up that piece and a dot of glue will hold it closed. Cover the rolled end with another small suede piece, fringed on both ends. Through the top loop it forms, connect it to the hole in the zipper tab with a little metal link. That link came off a broken necklace and needle-nose pliers from Fiskars pinched it back together.

Before I get hundreds of calls to ask where to get the pastel fur let me tell you.

Donna Salyers
Fabulous Furs
700 Madison Avenue
Covington, KY 41011
(606) 291-3300

Long Scarves

So often after cutting out a blouse or dress there is a long narrow piece of fabric left over. The perfect solution for wonderful usage is a scarf, if the fabric is thin and silky. One was worn in program 1405 with the pin woven vest and made from two left over fabrics. The other was worn in this program. The scrap sizes were different so here are the results of both.

The two sided scarf from 1405 was a chiffon layer on one side, an elaborately woven pattern in metallics on the other. Very light and transparent, they made a nice reversible accessory - two scarves in one. Pin the two layers together all around while flat on a table as they are very slippery and shift easily. After pinning trim them together so both are exactly the same size. There is nothing sacred about their 11" x 68" size. One of the scraps happened to be of those dimensions so they were both cut that size.

Stitch all around in a scant 1/4" seam, leaving an opening at one end large enough for your hand. Use a lightweight thread, if these fabrics are very thin, such as Coats and Clark very fine or even thin rayon embroidery thread. Cut off the corners, turn it right side out, press edges. Close the opening with hand stitches.

The 1410 scarf wasn't a scrap, but a 1/2 yard purchase of 45" silk chiffon with a streaky hand dyed look. To make it long enough to hang gracefully, an 8" piece of a heavy weight silk charmeuse (from the accompanying blouse) was added to each end. Not only does this extend it to about 60", but also it acts as ballast. Fold it in half lengthwise, wrong side out. Stitch the three open sides except for a turning opening. Cut off corner, turn, press, handstitch closed. Check the prices of similar scarves in expensive shops. Astonishing!!

Loom Wovens

Working with hand woven fabric is a very special event. For those of us who are not weavers, think what this process means. Very laboriously, a loom must first be warped. That is choosing all these wonderful heartwrenchingly beautiful yarns. Attach hundreds of them to the warp beam, thread each through the heddle eyes that lift or lower yarns as weaving progresses. The actual weaving takes place as the woof or filling yarn(s) is woven, as the shuttle goes back and forth, and alternate yarns lift and lower. At first glance, these fabrics may seem expensive, but consider the process: labor and logic intensive, time consuming to create, plus the expense of purchasing all those gorgeous yarns. This makes it a special use fabric only, but most definitely worth the cost.

Because these fabrics are so precious, they require more than average thought, planning and construction of garments from them. Without careful consideration, you waste your time, and monetary investment, not to mention the beautiful fabric an artist has labored to provide. Thus this project started as more a mental exercise than a physical one. Before cutting into the limited amount of yardage I made very sure I had carefully considered every facet of the project, because only the best effort is good enough.

For starters I steam pressed the fabric. Although I suspected the artist (who I know) had already pre-shrunk it, but I didn't want to leave anything to chance.

Pattern pieces of conventional shapes will not fit on my limited amount of fabric so I am using some oddly shaped pattern pieces. On doubled fabric they aren't going to fit. I will instead cut out single layers. To ensure ALL pieces fit, cut a duplicate pattern so everything can be laid out singly. In any fabric shop you can purchase a fibrous pattern tracer or pattern paper from which to trace and cut this duplicate.

For years I've been telling you everything is possible from a basic pattern. When the standard pieces, front, back and sleeve, won't fit on the allotted fabric, it's time to add pieces together or split pieces apart. To get this straight in my head

figuring out how it can work, I play around with miniature patterns until it all works. This result can then be duplicated in full size. Here's an example of how to begin from a Bonfit patterner. The basic shapes come from their book which accompanies the adjustable patterner.

Step one.
Front with cut on sleeve panel
Extend the sleeve to wrist.
Draw a raglan line underarm to neck.

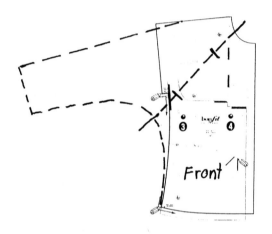

Back with cut on sleeve plus
higher neck.
Extend the sleeve to wrist.

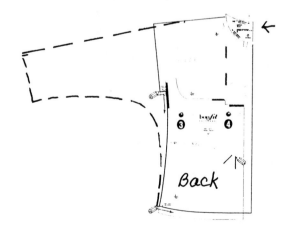

Step two:

Cut sleeve off front at raglan line.

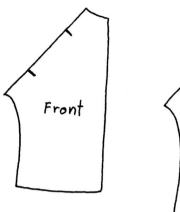

Tape front sleeve section ot back sleeve.

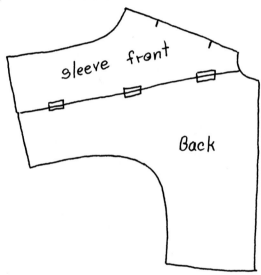

Step three:

Remember a basic, a sloper, an adjustable patterner has no seams. To complete, simply add seams and hems where needed, center front extension for buttons and buttonholes.

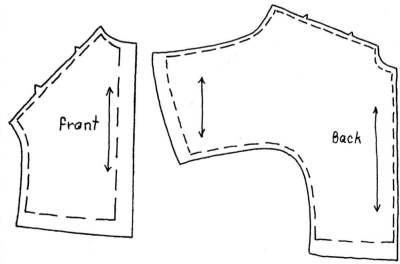

Step four:

Cut out facings and lining. This is simply deciding where a line will go where facing and lining join. At that line add a seam to each.

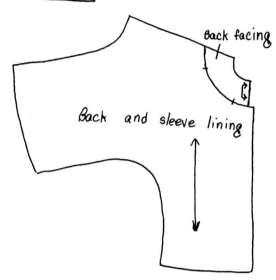

I laid the pieces on the fabric in what seemed the best fit, and most economical use of yardage. It is always a good idea to take a break, then come back for a second look before cutting. I am so glad I did, because I made the shocking discovery that I had 2 left fronts and 2 left backs.

Truly, I couldn't tell right from wrong sides on this particular fabric, but if possible I'd rather use one side consistently. Also, lightly smooth your hand up and down to see if there's a nap. Nap needs to go in the down direction, if there is a difference.

The only way my oddly shaped pattern pieces would work is to piece the sleeves. If a seam must go somewhere, you have two choices; either a straight grain seam on the diagonal of the sleeve, but with an invisible joining. Choice two is to cut a line parallel with the wrist edge that would produce a bias joining. Choice #1 is the most logical. I do keep reminding you that sewing is for intelli-

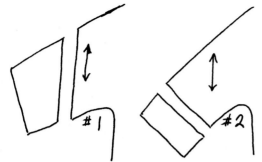

gent people! Much thought is involved and hasty decisions will be regretted.

There will be no fabric for facings unless pieced. I have a machine woven wool of a similar color that could be used. I opted for piecing the long front facing and using all the fabric possible. The only contrast fabric necessary will be the sleeve false hems (facings), and on that I may couch some raveled out yarns of the original fabric scraps. An alternative is to cut these sleevefacings slightly off grain. Will it matter on the inside of the sleeve? Not really. As it turned out, because the sleeve is bias instead of straight cut, the fabric hung out long enough to turn up for a hem and the facing I had prepared wasn't even used.

Here is the layout that worked best with the sleeve extensions cut off. Remember to add seams at those cuts so they can be sewn together. The resulting seam on this fabric is invisible. Hand woven fabrics are frequently narrower widths. This one is only 34", thus all the juggling. When wools are usually 60", I was thrilled to be able to get this out of only 2 1/2 yards of such narrow fabric.

Once cut, the next hurdle will be interfacings. Because this wool and mohair hand woven is soft and spongy, a lightweight woven interfacing will be fused to the entire backside of the fabric. This will make it more crisp for this tailored project. It will also reinforce it since handwovens are looser in yarn closeness than machine wovens. The woven fusible chosen is extremely lightweight, similar to a cotton batiste. At back and front neckline and down the center front where buttons and buttonholes will be, fuse a heavier interfacing layer to the fabric back before the batiste layer is added.

There will be welt pockets, therefore its reasonable to have matching bound buttonholes. In a tightly woven hard finished fabric I would do

this. In this handwoven, the tiny narrow buttonhole lips would be in danger of unravelling, despite the fusible. Machine stitched buttonholes are safer. Don't ignore the possibility of other fas-

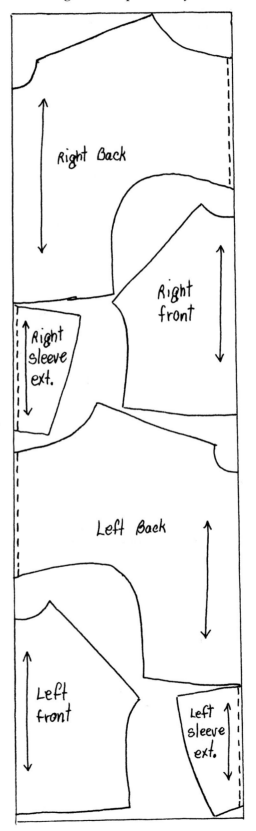

tenings. Buttonloops in tubes of complimentary fabric or something completely unique would be great.

With this fabric I wanted a slippery lining. Remember you can always do this even though you don't have a pattern for one. The lining is simply identical to the outer garment, minus the neck and front facings, plus two seam allowances where lining and facing are joined. Let's put that in picture form for clarity.

Draw on the pattern a line about where the front facing should be.

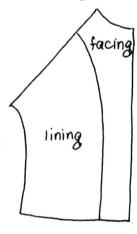

It would look about like this. Two ways are suggested how this could be cut out in fabrics. One way would be to trace this pattern on another paper or on a pattern tracer. Cut the two apart on the dotted line. Lay the facing on the fashion fabric and cut out adding a 5/8" seam at the dotted line. Do the same with the lining piece, again adding the seam allowance.

The second way is to only use the original pattern without duplicating it. Where you have drawn the line for facing edge, put a line of straight pins attaching the facing to the fashion fabric. Cut out the front edge and neckline. Turn the unit over, and using a seam gauge, cut the fabric 5/8" wider, being careful to cut through the fabric only, not the paper pattern. Repeat the same process on the lining fabric adding the seam allowance on the opposite side of the marked line.

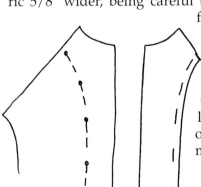

Repeat the process on the back pattern for the neck facing and lining. Remember they will stitch together on the shoulders, so be sure to have the facings an equal width there. The more you work

with slight pattern changes such as this, the easier and more logical patterns become. But you must keep your brain awake. You must think ahead to determine what to do and how it will work.

For finishing details think what possibilities there are for giving it an extra special touch. I only had a few very small scraps left from my piece of hand woven fabric. Here are some of the extras I considered:

Piping all around the front and neck edges of UltraSuede, FabuLeather, or bias cut silk might be very pretty. There are many skirts, pants, blouses, vests in my collection that can be worn with this coat. To add that little trim might somewhat limit its versatility.

In a treasure drawer were several cords, yarns, novelty threads, and beads in similar colors. Could they compliment it for a more spectacular overall look? Give this careful consideration. This is a wonderful fabric, one of a kind, woven by an artist. I chose a pattern with simple, spare lines to allow the fabric to take center stage. You are collaborating with this artist when you add your work to hers. Would adding any outside embellishments be as big a mistake as painting a mustache on the Mona Lisa? If the answer is yes, then stick with the fabric and its yarns only. Here are some suggestions for doing just that.

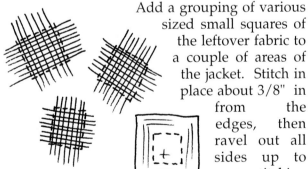

Add a grouping of various sized small squares of the leftover fabric to a couple of areas of the jacket. Stitch in place about 3/8" in from the edges, then ravel out all sides up to your stitching line.

Cut strips about 1" wide. Ravel out about 1/2" along one long side. Turn under the other edge and press. Zigzag these on the garment in some interesting arrangements.

Ravel out several long yarns from a scrap. Either by hand  or attached to a bobbin on your machine's bobbin winder, twist these together to make a thick cord. When they are so tightly twisted they start to back twist, put a finger on the center forcing the backwind uniformly. Tie the ends in a knot and the cord will stay twisted. These lovely cords of the fabric's own yarns can be used as a trim around the neck or front edge, as buttonloops. My scraps were too short for this.

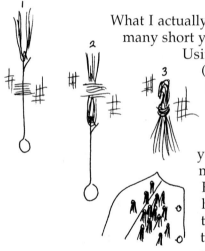 What I actually did was ravel out many short yarns about 4" long. Using a latch hook (also called a tube turner, found in notions departments), I poked it under a few yarns in my garment and again out. Fold a short yarn in half and catch it on the hook. Pull it through the fabric so a big loop hangs down. Detach the latch hook, put yarn ends through the loop and pull snugly in place, creating a little tassel. A whole grouping of these are on one shoulder area of my garment. If at any time I decide they look a bit much, nothing is permanently lost or ruined. They can all be pulled out to revert to plain fabric.

See photo 1411a on page 49.

Out of her handwoven wool, Wendy Hahn of Richland, Washington made a wonderful bomber with flanges on the shoulder. This is combined with a blending of heavy cotton sleeves and collar and all machine embroidered in the same color threads as in the handwoven fabric. Incidentally, this jacket is the patternless one made at the end of series 11 where the sleeves zipout to become a vest.

See photo 1411b on page 49.

 This brown wool vest by June Greig of St. Louis is not a handwoven but has the look of one. Primitive people are painted in the background with a ballpoint pen! A lot of shredded yarns from the fabric are couched here and there with some subtle beads and a little embroidery of metallic cords. The buttonholes are stitched over two patches of fabric, then simply raveled out to the stitching line.

Working with handwoven fabric is a luxurious, rewarding experience. Plan and execute the garment carefully in a timeless style to get many years of pleasure from wearing it.

The Clutch

Back in series 8 was a program called Platter Purses, so named because a meat platter was actually used for the purse shape. There have been a lot of requests for more as these are such fun to make. It only takes a little fabric, and any shred of fabric can be used. It is very quick to make the basic bag. The embellishments could take a little or a lot of time.

See photo 1412 on page 52.

I must warn you that these little beauties are addictive! Make one and a whole lot of other ideas for more pop into your head. To make the next several a lot faster, I have a stack of the inner structure cut out ready to go.

As a rule, a small clutch bag like this doesn't hold very much and would therefore be a dressy or special occasion accessory. Nothing sacred about the small size, it could be enlarged if that better suits your needs. Add a shoulder strap so it can be worn rather than carried. Just like any article of clothing, this can be adapted in whatever manner you choose.

Think of the special occasions for which these bags would be useful. If someone in your family is going to a prom or a party, maybe this little accessory would be just the right touch. For weddings you could mass produce many of these quickly for all the bridesmaids. Holiday seasons provide reasons to carry these. If you produce more than you have any use for, they're very

saleable items to donate to the next club or church bazaar.

Here on a small scale is the purse pattern. 1/8" equals 1" in the full sized bag. When finished it is folded like an envelope and its dimensions are about 10 1/2" wide, 5 1/2" high. If a full size pattern is easier for you to use, we have one for sale at The Sewing Connection office. It has complete directions for the 10 different bags photographed together as seen in this chapter. In that pattern are included three different styles with several variations for each. View A is a tri-fold, an envelope style whose pattern you see here. The bottom straight edge folds up, and is stitched in place. The top curved edge folds down for the flap.

View B has an extra front piece added before a large flap folds down. View C has one or more zippers. They all offer opportunities to use unique fabrics and trims and allow yourself unlimited artistic license. View A, the envelope bag will be covered here with several more decorative ideas suggested and explained, different from the pattern.

There are four layers in this bag. The outer layer is the fashion fabric. Anything can be used for this but think of practicality. It is unlikely that you will either wash or dry clean the finished bag, although you certainly could if you so desire. For this reason hard-finished fabrics might be more sensible since they are more soil resistant. Any of the manmade suedes and leathers are ideal for these bags. Other good choices are bengaline, taffeta, brocade, satin, or velvet for dressy occasions. Upholstery fabrics like tapestry and jacquards are reasonable choices. Some of these fabrics are so decorative in themselves that they will need no other embellishment.Plain fabrics offer the perfect background for the stitching, trims, beads, etc. you may want to add to others.

The second layer is a fusible fleece and it will be fused to the fashion fabric's backside to beef it up. It will make the outer fabric appropriately stiff and sturdy as a quality bag needs. This is the only layer I actually cut out using the pattern. For the other layers I just want rectangles of fabric

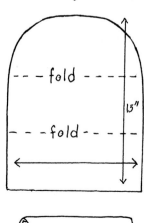

slightly larger. This eliminates the necessity of having everything cut so precisely that the fusible material will pose no threat to iron or ironing board. Also to cut only the one fleece layer is a little quicker. Craft fleece is found in the shop interfacing department on a large bolt by the yard. Sometimes they carry it in pre-measured folded lengths in sealed packages. There are a few major brands of this readily available. Their thickness is between 1/8" up to 1/4" which mashes down somewhat when fused. This thin firm fleece works very well to turn any fabric into a nice firmness and any hefty fleece or batting would not be suitable.

The third layer is a fusible interfacing which will be attached to the lining wrong side. Ordinarily a lining in a garment, if interfaced at all, would only want a very sheer interfacing. This is not true of this little bag which will profit by the firmness of a sturdier interfacing. For this I prefer the same heavy duty fusible of a weft insertion type construction I use in tailoring suits.

The inner layer is lining and it may be any sort of fabric sold as lining. It may also be any print or solid fabric in my stash large enough to cover this 11" x 15" rectangle needed. Sometimes leftover blouse or dress fabrics are good in a silky type. Rayon or wool challis or crepes appear in others. Anything is fair game. The only requirement is that it color coordinate with the outer fashion fabric layer. It needs to pull the whole project together, and this is something color does very well. Some of these little bags are self-fabric lined. It is certainly fine to use the same fabric inside and out.

To begin, collect all your fabrics and then think about what trims would add to the total look. Novelty threads and cords, beads, and decorative buttons could all make it look complete. Other trim fabrics could be interesting and allow coordinating with more garments. Complete your plans.

To begin construction the first decision is whether or not the outside fabric will be textured or used in its flat state. If pleating, tucking, wrinkling or otherwise manipulating the fabric, this is the time to do it before fusing the backing. Some of these techniques use a lot of fabric, others only a little, beyond the pattern measurements. Be pre-

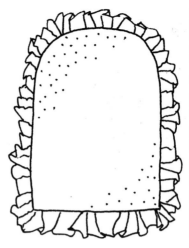

pared with excess fabric in advance to cover your needs. The usual way to wrinkle a small piece of fabric is to wet it, wring it out so multiple wrinkles appear and press it dry, wrong side up, pressing the wrinkles in place. Cut the fusible fleece with your pattern and place it over the wrinkled fabric with the fusible side down. Cover with a press cloth and fuse with a steam iron for a good bond. If your steam is not profuse, spray the cloth with a spray bottle of tapwater and press further until there is a firm bonding. Firmness here is a desirable quality for a truly professional look. If you only partially press it with a puffy quality to it, it looks homemade. A really good job is of prime importance.

Pleating or tucking are other texturizing options you might consider before fusing the fleece. If the joining of several fabrics appeals to you, look into chapter 13 to consider a crazy quilt technique. Or think how pretty the Fiskars novelty rotary blades cut suede strips could be all overlapped and fused to the fleece. I've used the wave blade from chapter 8 on  many strips in variations and shades of red, magenta, burgundy for a really vibrant combination.

Another alternative is to fuse this fleece to the back of a plain fabric and embellish it to your hearts content. Many of you have embroidery capabilities on your sewing machines. Here is the perfect opportunity to thread paint a picture of your choice. Coats and Clark's new 30 weight embroidery rayon is really pretty done in any of the designs my Memorycraft 9000 memory cards have to offer.   If you have some of these you haven't yet tried, don't waste the trial on throw-away scraps. These small projects are not only perfect for any design, but also make useful gifts. Every effort should be put to good use. Also try the new twist thread for some interesting blending looks. In the metallic threads the same designs are very dressy.

If you haven't any embroidery capability, you surely have several decorative stitches which are also pretty to use in great profusion over the fabric surface. If your machine does anything fancier than straight stitch, you have decorative potential which would be a challenge to try.

The next step is to put right sides together of the embellished outside and the interfaced lining. Pin in a few places and stitch a shallow 1/4" seam all around the fleece shape, leaving an opening on the flat end of about 5". Trim close to the line

except at the opening. Leaving a more generous seam allowance here will make it easier to tuck in when turned. Around the curved end a pinking blade or pinking shears will both trim and notch it at the same time.

Turn right side out and press the edge very flat. If necessary use a clapper to get a really

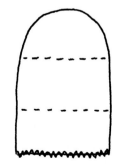

crisp edge. Using monofilament thread both on top and in the bobbin, zigzag the flat end in stitches as narrow as possible. Divide the piece in thirds by folding. Mark the fold which will be the purse bottom with a couple of pins.

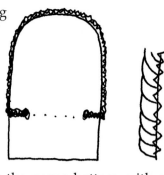

From that 1/3 point, all around the curved end zigzag a decorative cord in harmonizing color. This both makes the finished bag look very professional and makes the edge even more crisp. This cord is found in trim departments or sometimes in drapery supplies. Zigzag this on as narrow as 1.5 or 2. Use a multipurpose foot. Do this with the lining side up, right side down. Lay the cord end an inch or so into the fold before attaching to the bag edge around to the opposite corresponding point.

Now fold up the lower flat third and zigzag each end. Attach a fastener or a snap, Velcro or a button and your bag is finished. This is not only a fun little project everyone can do easily, it is also the perfect opportunity to do something more decorative or more extravagant than you would probably do on an article of clothing.

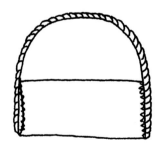

St. Louis Symphony   Chapter 13

To those of us who dearly love beautiful fabrics, a small piece of something wonderful can spur a whole wardrobe! Such was a fabric I saw in St. Louis. Some fabrics are lovely on their own, in an isolated situation. One is an "invitational" fabric, one which invites you to combine several other fabrics with it for endless matches. A crazy quilt actually, pastel tints of green, aqua, lavender, aubergine silk shantung in odd shapes of about 4" in size were all combined on a gauze backing. Quite pricey, but there was a good reason! Silk shantung is the designer's darling right now so that in itself is appealing. But beyond that this is all decoratively and elaborately stitched at every joining. This all says we have something important and unusual, not just another run of the mill piece.

As I carried the bolt around and it extended its invitation, other fabrics wanting to join the party included an aqua UltraSuede. Two different pieces of silk charmeuse exactly matched one or another of the patches. A wool gabardine blended with a pale green. My mind recalled items in my closets already made that would be likely matches. In my many travels I'm certain to see a linen or silk suiting to round it out. A silk fabric like this knows no season and can be combined with anything for year round wear.

Once you determine you must have that unusual piece the next decision is how much of it. This depends on what you are going to make of it and all its coordinates. Sometimes these decisions are obvious and instantaneous. Sometimes it pays to deliberate and not be too hasty. My first thought with this silk patchwork was a coat to wear for a formal occasion. How many of those situations occur and how much wear would it get? Let's be more realistic.

From that very large garment down to a small one - a vest suddenly seemed most logical. Considering all the other fabrics plus garments existing at home, a vest is the only logical choice. There are jacket fabrics that would go over it so I didn't want a jacket. Several blouses in solids would go under it so making a blouse would be senseless and besides, it really isn't supple enough for a blouse. Pants and skirts could come from coordinates. Yes, a vest is the right garment, so 3/4 of a yard of the crazy quilt would be just right.

That fabric shopping was fun but the best part is yet to come. Notions! Carry the cut folded fabric to the notions area and see what treasures are available, braids, trims - I can't resist. I buy whenever I see them. Because I stick to the same color families, everything always matches up with something else and it will eventually be used. Some prefer to buy only what they will need to use immediately, avoiding home storage. Others of us are collectors and feel "we pass this way but once". If we see it, buy it as we may never see that treasure again!

I save this dessert course for last, savoring this special treat. Depending on what I find I'll decide to button that vest asymmetrically because three large buttons are perfect for it. Or maybe a bunch of little buttons suggest a high jewel neck with silken button loops all the way down. Maybe a breathtaking braid will become a neckline border with a single large button. Or perhaps some other drop-dead baubles inspire a frog type closure. A quick trip to a <u>good</u> fabric shop is an impossibility as I want many hours there to really explore and find the best, drink in the wonder, learn, and feel my creativity recharging. If for any fabric I can't find unique finishing touches, I won't get anything. When I get home the best choices may already be there, filed away in bank check boxes, each box housing a different color choice of buttons.

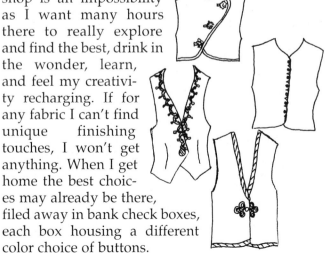

Could you produce your own crazy quilt fabric similar to this? Yes, of course, given time. You'll quickly realize why the purchased version is expensive.

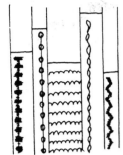

These types of silks which will go into the restructured fabric are usually quite ravelly. On series 8 I found a jacket made of many pieces of thin scarf weight silks can be fragile. This piecing involved 1/4" seams and the pieced fabric was then backed by a firm lightweight batting. Even though a lot of decorative stitching firmed up and strengthened the whole piece enormously, the actual seams pulled loose in places of the most strain. Had decorative stitching been done directly on the seams rather than in the interiors of each piece, this wouldn't happen.

To actually make seams is possible but I noticed in my purchased crazy quilt, several corners were odd shapes and looked like no seaming was done prior to decorative stitching. Despite this, raw edges would need to be turned under. Fusing might be the best way. A good base could be a fusible tricot or a woven equally lightweight fusible.

To prepare all the patches, cut these pieces any shape you want and of the size you want. Put your vest pattern in the interfacing and place one on the ironing board, fusible side up.

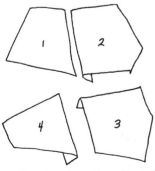

Play around with the patches first to get a feel for doing this before fusing. The first piece may be laid on an edge, in a corner, or in the center. You will then work away from it, covering up a raw edge with each successive piece placed. Each of the pieces after the first flat one will need an edge pressed under before overlapping a raw edge.

When all pieces are fused to the vest interfacing shapes, decoratively stitch over each folded edge to permanently secure it in place. Here is a great opportunity to use all those automatic stitches your machine will do.

Because I already had the purchased crazy quilt fabric for the vest, I did all this on fusible fleece instead, in a rectangle 12" x 18". This will later be made into a handbag - probably a clutch from program 1412. Had it been on a lightweight fusible, it would need to be backed by a stabilizer or clamped in a hoop to hold the fabric out flat and taut for the decorative stitching. Since it was all completed on the rectangle of fleece it was firm and stiff, so no additional aid is needed for the stitching.

I chose the dense patterns on the machine as I like the look of lushness. To heighten this even more, Coats and Clark's new 30 weight rayon embroidery thread was used in a strong bright pink. On the silk pieces ranging from purple through magenta, fuscia, geranium red, red-orange, the intense 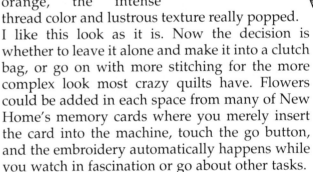 thread color and lustrous texture really popped. I like this look as it is. Now the decision is whether to leave it alone and make it into a clutch bag, or go on with more stitching for the more complex look most crazy quilts have. Flowers could be added in each space from many of New Home's memory cards where you merely insert the card into the machine, touch the go button, and the embroidery automatically happens while you watch in fascination or go about other tasks.

Another crazy quilt direction would be to change the thread to metallic glitz in pink or red and border the rayon thick lines with delicate filigree design lines. Today's machines and thread varieties deliver such marvellous possibilities the combinations are endless. If a large number of sewers were all given the same equipment to operate the same fabrics, the same threads, the choices are so vast no two projects would turn out the same.

Manmade suede or leather would also make a good crazy quilt piece for a bag. A pattern was first drawn for this with curvy lines everywhere. This was cut apart and each piece used as a pattern to cut out in suede. No ravelling can happen on these edges so they needn't be turned under, merely butted together. All these pieces in blues and greens are fused to the same size fusible fleece for another bag.

To give all these touching edges a finished look, 3/8" crosswise strips of suede were cut with a Fiskars pinking blade either in a hand held cutter or since the lines are straight, in the craft cutter attached to a wide ruler. Lengthwise cut suede strips wouldn't do as they have no stretch. Because of the crosswise stretch, these smoothly curve while you stitch them down in place. Eventually lots of little buttons and beads will be grouped around on this.

Still another type of crazy quilt variation was seen on a vest on the cover of The Sewing Connection - Book 11. This was a big grouping of oddly shaped pieces in different tints and shades of a blue-purple cotton. They had all been twin-needle pintucked in parallel rows to look like farmers' plowed fields from the air. They were then all bordered by trees and shrubbery to cover over the raw edges and connect the fields. This was mohair yarn in variegated colors from turquoise to blue to purple couched on with monofilament thread so no stitches showed. The wonderful device, which makes this possible holds the yarn up close to the needle while you zigzag over it, is called a Miracle Stitcher. The feed dog is dropped and you can stitch in any direction. This is sold by Janome - New Home machine dealers and will only fit New Home machines. A wonderful gadget!

See Photo 1413a Page 52

Another crazy quilt shown on this program was a fun holiday outfit from Kathy Ongelmeyer of St. Ann, MO. It was a green velvet long skirt topped by the vest in metallics, lace, silks, velvets, all bordered by elaborate stitching, braids and trims for a very festive mood.

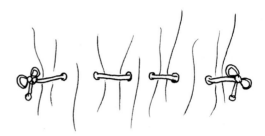

The back of my vest is shaped in at the waist by stitching 9 eyelets in a row, each about 11 1/2" apart - or more or less as long as it's an even number. Through these a bias tube of silk is laced to gather it up slightly. This tube is tied in a little bow at each end to hold it in place. More of this tubing is handstitched down the right front to form buttonloops.

See Photo 1413b Page 52

Despite the fact that this fabric is a crazy quilt, its subdued colors make it a very serene garment. You see it here surrounded by some of my harmonizing pieces crowded around it in crazy quilt fashion. You can see how, like an orchestra conductor, it pulls together all or any of the surrounding pieces to produce a wardrobe symphony!

Go a little crazy yourself and add some spice to your wardrobe, incorporating a lot of the ideas I've been showing you. This was the last program of series 14 and I'm now off and running to bring more fresh thoughts back to you.

The goal of The Sewing Connection is to connect you with other sewers who can inspire your work, to bring you techniques to elevate your quality and to convince you that you really can do it.

If you have fun with The Sewing Connection, write or call the management of your public television station and request that they air series 15 coming up soon. Until then I want you to know that - just like you - I absolutely love to sew. Enjoy!!